Tourism Destinations Southern Africa

Heather du Plessis

JUTA

1853

First published 2000

ISBN 0 7021 5272 2

Editing: Pat Hanekom
Maps: Cath Crookes
Cover design: Pumphaus Design Studio
Book design and DTP: Charlene Bate
Printed in South Africa by Creda Communications, Eliot Avenue, Epping

Acknowledgements

Many thanks are due:

South African Airways and Sun International for use of their photo libraries

Corinne Hitching (Green Globe, London), Sonja Grünbauer (SAA) and Janet Allison (SAA) for photographic contributions

Pansy Mekwa for comments on the cultural aspects of various population groups

Nicola Wakelin-Theron (TSA) and my commissioning editor, Pranill Ramchander, for suggestions and ideas during the developmental stage of the book

Louis, my husband, and my son Francois for support and understanding during the many hours spent on the compilation of this book.

Errors

Although the author and publisher have made every effort to ensure that the information contained in this book was correct at the time of going to press, the author and publisher do not assume, and hereby disclaim, any liability to any party for any damage or loss caused by errors, omissions or misleading information.

Preface

In the recent publication, *South Africa's Travel and Tourism, Economic Driver for the 21st Century*, the World Travel and Tourism Council identified education and training as a prerequisite for the country's success in the global tourism industry.

In writing this book, I have endeavoured to provide an essential tool for students and travel consultants who may have little knowledge of southern African destinations. The book highlights South Africa's most important tourist destinations, enabling readers to easily identify key tourist attractions. At the same time it provides an insight into the multi-ethnic cultural heritage of South Africa, as well as an appreciation of its stand towards conservation and eco-tourism. With the exception of Chapter 1, there is an activity at the end of each chapter, which should be of particular benefit to students and even of assistance to travel consultants.

The first chapter of the book covers an introduction by way of an overview of South Africa, followed by individual chapters on each of the nine provinces. Attention is given to the main tourist attractions, cultural, sport and leisure activities within each area. Separate chapters are devoted to each of the neighbouring countries of Lesotho, Swaziland, Namibia, Botswana and Zimbabwe.

Some of South Africa's provinces, such as KwaZulu-Natal and the Western Cape, are blessed with a diversity of tourist attractions impossible to condense into one chapter of a book of this nature. It was therefore necessary to selectively represent areas that offer a tremendous holiday experience. In such cases, as much comprehensive information as space allows, is given in the text.

At the time of going to press, the South African Government was about to offically rename the Anglo–Boer War from its familiar title (used in this book) to the more appropriate and nationally inclusive Anglo–Boer South African War.

Heather du Plessis
November 1999

Contents

Chapter 4

Wildlife Parks and Nature Reserves
Krugersdorp Nature Reserve, Lion Safari Park, Rhino and Lion Reserve,
Witwatersrand National Botanical Garden

Tourist Attractions

JOHANNESBURG

SOWETO

PRETORIA
Church Square, Union Buildings, Voortrekker Monument, National Zoological
Gardens, Premier Diamond Mine, The State Theatre

MAGALIESBERG

Historic Sites: Sterkfontein Caves, Wonder Cave

Cultural Villages: Lesidi Cultural Village, Sibaya, Phumangena Zulu Village,
Pioneer Open Air Museum

Chapter 5

Wildlife Parks and Nature Reserves
Kruger National Park, Private Game Reserves (Mala Mala, Sabi Sabi, Londolozi),
Gustav Klingbiel Nature Reserve, Mount Sheba Nature Reserve

Tourist Attractions

MPUMALANGA HIGHVELD
Loskop Dam and Nature Reserve, Botshabelo Mission Station

ESCARPMENT
Panorama Route, Blyde River Canyon, Pilgrim's Rest, Mac Mac Falls and
Mac Mac Pools, Long Tom Pass, Bourke's Luck Potholes, Lydenburg,
Lydenburg Heads, Dullstroom

LOWVELD
Sudwala Caves, Nelspruit

WETLAND REGION
Wakkerstroom

Cultural Villages: Tsonga Kraal (Hans Merensky Reserve), Ndebele Villages
(Loopspruit and Botshabelo), Swazi Cultural Village (Matsulu)

Chapter 9

x

INTRODUCTION TO SOUTH AFRICA

Facts at a Glance

Capital	Pretoria
Size	1 219 090 sq km
Population	40,5m
Currency	1 rand = 100 cents
Main Languages	English, Afrikaans, isiZulu, isiXhosa, isiNdebele, siSwati, sePedi, seSotho, xiTsonga, seTswana and tshiVenda
Main Religions	Christianity, Islam, Judaism, Hinduism, Buddhism and Indigenous Beliefs
Time Zone	GMT+2

Geographical Outline

The Republic of South Africa is located at the southern tip of Africa, bordering Namibia, Botswana and Zimbabwe to the north, Mozambique to the north-east, Swaziland to the east, and surrounding the Kingdom of Lesotho (a landlocked country) to the south-east. It has 2 798 kilometres of coastline and is bordered by the Atlantic Ocean to the west and the Indian Ocean to the east.

The land can be divided into two distinctive geographical regions – a high interior plateau known as the Highveld, which is separated from the narrow plain known as the Lowveld by the mountain ranges that form the Great Escarpment. Important ranges to be found within the country include the Soutpansberg, the Waterberg and Strydpoortberge in the north, the Drakensberg to the east, the Langeberg, Roggeveld-berge, Nuweveldberge, Swartberg, Outeniekwaberge, Kougaberge, Sneeuberge, Baviaanskloofberge, Grootrivierberge, Winterberge and Stormberge to the south.

The country's largest river system is the Orange River that rises in the Drakensberg Mountains and flows westward to the Atlantic Ocean. Other rivers are the Caledon, Vaal, Limpopo, Crocodile, Olifants, Tugela, Great Kei, Great Fish, Sundays, Breede and Berg rivers. The main storage dams are the Vaal, Bloemhof, Gariep, Theewaterskloof and Steenbras dams.

The country is prone to drought and much of the land is dry from lack of rain or evaporation. Altitude and rainfall patterns determine the diversity of vegetation.

Introduction

The Region

South Africa is one of the most beautiful countries in the world. It offers a wonderful climate, an immense cultural heritage, historical sights, numerous scenic attractions, an abundance of unique flora and some of the best game-viewing possibilities on the African continent. It has a good infrastructure, an excellent transportation network and world-class accommodation and resorts.

As a country it has much to offer to both domestic and international tourists. Due to its size and diversity, people can experience many different types of holiday depending upon the choice of region. Climate, vegetation and lifestyle vary to such an extent that it is possible to experience desert and wilderness, mountain and wetland, bushveld and the tropics all in one country.

The Economy

The nation's wealth is based largely on its natural resources. Main industries include mining, manufacturing and agriculture. It is the world's leading supplier of gold, chromium and platinum.

The Importance of Tourism

Tourism is an important sector in a nation's economy. The development of a successful tourism industry contributes to the creation of wealth, provides job opportunities and improves quality of life.

The majority of South Africa's tourists come from within the country itself, however, the past few years have seen a significant increase in international tourism, especially from Europe and the United States of America.

Climate

Factors such as latitude, altitude, wind and ocean currents play a significant role in the country's weather pattern. The western part of the land receives much less rain than the east and drought is common throughout the land. Despite a well-defined winter season, it is possible to enjoy sunshine in South Africa throughout the year.

Transportation and Accessibility

Road

South Africa's route network and infrastructure is one of the finest on the African continent, allowing for easy access to the nation's tourist attractions. The country's extensive road network is well signposted to facilitate touring on unfamiliar roads.

Numerous coach operators provide modern air-conditioned coaches to enable the tourist to commute between the country's main towns and cities, as well as to visit tourist attractions such as the Kruger National Park and Sun City. The three main operators are Greyhound, Inter-Cape Mainliner, and Translux.

Tourism Destinations Southern Africa

Car hire facilities are available at most South African airports as well as city centres. Major car hire companies are AVIS, Budget Rent A Car, Europcar, Hertz, Imperial Car Hire and Tempest Car Hire. A valid driver's licence is required for South African citizens and an international driving permit for foreign visitors. Most car hire companies set a minimum age of 23 years.

	BLOEMFONTEIN	CAPE TOWN	DURBAN	EAST LONDON	GABORONE	GRAHAMSTOWN	JOHANNESBURG	KIMBERLEY	MAPUTO	MASERU	MBABANE	PORT ELIZABETH	PRETORIA	WELKOM	WINDHOEK
BEAUFORT WEST	544	460	1178	605	1042	492	942	504	1349	609	1129	501	1000	697	1629
BLOEMFONTEIN		1004	634	584	622	601	398	177	897	157	677	677	456	153	1593
BRITSTOWN	398	710	1032	609	791	496	725	253	1289	555	1075	572	783	551	1378
CAPE TOWN	1004		1753	1099	1501	899	1402	962	1900	1160	1680	769	1460	1156	1500
COLESBERG	226	778	860	488	848	375	624	292	1123	383	903	451	682	379	1573
DE AAR	346	762	980	557	843	444	744	305	1243	503	1023	520	802	499	1430
DURBAN	634	1753		674	979	854	588	811	625	590	562	984	646	564	2227
EAST LONDON	584	1079	674		1206	180	982	780	1301	630	1238	310	1040	737	1987
GABORONE	622	1501	979	1206		1223	358	538	957	702	719	1299	350	579	1735
GEORGE	773	438	1319	645	1361	465	1171	762	1670	913	1450	335	1229	926	1887
GRAAFF REINET	424	787	942	395	1012	282	822	490	1321	599	1101	291	880	577	1697
GRAHAMSTOWN	601	899	854	180	1223		999	667	1478	692	1418	130	1057	754	1856
HARRISMITH	328	1331	306	822	673	929	282	505	649	284	468	1068	332	258	1921
JOHANNESBURG	398	1402	588	982	358	999		472	599	438	361	1075	58	258	1801
KEETMANSHOOP	1088	995	1722	1482	1230	1351	1296	911	1895	1245	1657	1445	1354	1205	505
KIMBERLEY	177	962	811	780	538	667	472		1071	334	833	743	530	294	1416
KLERKSDORP	288	1271	764	872	334	889	164	308	763	368	525	1009	222	145	1693
KROONSTAD	211	1214	537	795	442	812	187	339	742	247	522	888	245	71	1724
LADYSMITH	410	1413	236	752	755	932	364	587	567	366	386	1062	422	340	2008
MAFIKENG	464	1343	821	1048	158	1065	287	380	886	544	648	1141	294	321	1577
MAPUTO	897	1900	625	1301	957	1478	599	1071		853	223	1609	583	813	2400
MASERU	157	1160	590	630	702	692	438	334	853		633	822	488	249	1750
MBABANE	677	1680	562	1238	719	1418	361	833	223	633		1548	372	451	2162
MESSINA	928	1932	1118	1512	696	1529	530	1002	725	960	808	1605	472	788	2331
NELSPRUIT	757	1762	707	1226	672	1358	355	827	244	713	173	1434	322	639	2156
OUDTSHOORN	743	506	1294	704	1241	532	1141	703	1705	959	1417	394	1199	896	1828
PIETERMARITZBURG	555	1674	79	595	900	775	509	732	706	511	640	905	567	485	2148
PIETERSBURG	717	1721	907	1301	485	1318	319	791	605	749	515	1394	261	577	2120
PORT ELIZABETH	677	769	984	310	1299	130	1075	743	1609	822	1548		1133	830	1950
PRETORIA	456	1460	646	1040	350	1057	58	530	583	488	372	1133		316	1859
QUEENSTOWN	377	1069	676	207	999	269	775	554	1302	423	1240	399	833	525	1829
UMTATA	570	1314	439	235	1192	415	869	747	1064	616	1003	545	928	718	2066
UPINGTON	588	894	1222	982	730	851	796	411	1395	745	1157	945	854	669	2005
WELKOM	153	1156	564	737	479	754	258	294	813	249	451	830	316		1679
WINDHOEK	1593	1500	2227	1987	1735	1856	1801	1416	2400	1750	2162	1950	1859	1679	

▷ *Distances are measured in kilometres*

4

Border Crossings

There are numerous border crossings between South Africa and its neighbouring countries. The main posts are as follows:

Lesotho: Ficksburgbrug (24 hours), Maserubrug (24 hours), Sani Pass (08:00–16:00)
Swaziland: Golela (07:00–22:00), Oshoek (07:00–22:00), Mahamba (07:00–22:00)
Botswana: Ramatlabama (07:00–20:00), Kopfontein (07:00–22:00), Derdepoort (07:00–19:00), Swartkopfonteinhek (07:00–19:00), Stockpoort (08:00–18:00) and Groblersbrug (08:00–18:00)
Zimbabwe: Beit Bridge (05:30–22:30)
Mozambique: Manhoca (08:00–17:00), Lebombo (06:00–19:00), Lomahasha (07:00–17:00)
Namibia: Ariamsvlei (24 hours), Noordoewer (24 hours), Oranjemund (08:00–17:00), Velloorsdrif (08:00–22:00), Hohlweg (08:00–22:00), Klein Menasse (08:00–22:00)

Air

South Africa is served by numerous international carriers and offers direct links to Europe, North and South America, Australia, Asia and the Middle East, as well as an extensive regional network and domestic connections to most main centres within South Africa. There are three international airports – Johannesburg, Durban and Cape Town – and a regular shuttle service runs between these airports and city centres.

▷ *A South African Airways (SAA) passenger aircraft flying over Durban*

Rail

Regular scheduled mainline passenger train services operate between all major cities as well as into the neighbouring state of Zimbabwe.

Two world-renowned trains offer visitors a chance to view the country's magnificent scenery by rail, in five-star luxury. The Blue Train, considered to be one of the world's ultimate train experiences, transports its passengers between Cape Town and Pretoria, Cape Town and Port Elizabeth, Pretoria and Hoedspruit, and Pretoria and Victoria Falls. The luxurious Rovos Rail–Pride of Africa operates between Cape Town and Pretoria via Matjiesfontein and Kimberley, Pretoria and Victoria Falls, Pretoria and Komatipoort, with a road transfer to Skukuza, and from Cape Town to Knysna.

▷ *The Blue Train*

Visa Requirements

A valid passport is required for all visitors to South Africa and proof of sufficient funds or evidence of a return ticket may be requested. Most foreign nationals are exempt from visa requirements.

Accommodation

South Africa offers all categories of accommodation to suit every requirement, from first class hotels, wildlife lodges and resorts, timeshare, guesthouses, guest farms, bed and breakfast, backpackers' hostels, thatched rondavels, holiday flats and self-catering accommodation to caravan and camping facilities. A voluntary National Grading and Classification Scheme was introduced in 1994.

Most of the first class resorts offer a wide variety of sport and recreation facilities such as golf, tennis, squash, bowls and swimming.

Health

Precautions (prophylactic medication or vaccination) are recommended against the following diseases when travelling in South Africa:

▶ Malaria in the regions of Northern Province, Mpumalanga and the northern areas of KwaZulu-Natal;

▶ Yellow Fever if the traveller is over one year of age and has arrived from an infected area;

▶ Cholera for visitors to rural areas. Immunisation is not a prerequisite for entry into South Africa, but as an infectious disease cholera may pose a risk in certain areas.

Rabies is present in certain areas of the country and anyone who is bitten by an animal should immediately seek medical assistance. Bilharzia is common in the northern and eastern regions of the country, where visitors should avoid swimming in rivers and dams that may be contaminated. Tap water is considered safe to drink in urban areas, but precautions should be taken when travelling to rural areas.

Historic Highlights

The first inhabitants of South Africa were the San (hunter-gatherers) and the Khoikhoi (herders) who settled in the area several thousand years ago. The migration of people from the north into the country started around AD1400 and extended over a period covering several centuries.

In 1652 the Dutch East India Company established a supply station at the Cape for their ships sailing between Europe and the Far East. Fresh produce and water as well as health care were provided.

In 1657 the Company allowed its servants to become independent farmers (Free Burghers). The number of Dutch at the Cape greatly increased and they were joined in 1688 by a group of French Huguenots, fleeing anti-Protestant legislation in France.

Between 1795–1803 the Cape was controlled by the British, after which it returned to Dutch control from 1803–1806. In 1806 it was conquered again by the British who were given sovereignty of the Colony as a result of the European Peace Settlement. The expansion of the settlement led to confrontation with the Xhosa and Khoikhoi people over grazing and land.

In an effort to solve the Eastern Cape's frontier problems between the Xhosa and Boers (South Africans of mainly Dutch descent), the British moved the Xhosa out of the area, and in 1820 established a permanent new British settlement. Attempts to create a border between the settlers and Xhosa failed. However, the arrival of the British, whose attitude differed greatly from that of the Dutch, had a significant impact on the region.

British rule brought an end to slavery. The Boer settlers of the Eastern Cape frontier region were unhappy about their loss of slave labour and felt a lack of support from the British with regard to the continual cattle raiding by Xhosa. Many families set out in search of new land outside of British jurisdiction. Between 1835–1840 thousands of people left the Cape and headed for the interior in what was to become known as the Great Trek. Included in their number were Boers from the Western Cape.

The region which the Voortrekkers (pioneers) were moving into was inhabited by several African chiefdoms, who at that time were experiencing the effects of one of their most devastating periods of history known as the *Mfecane* (Ngune) or *Difaqane* (seSotho). In 1815 the Zulu chief, Shaka, established himself as head of the Zulu nation, transforming his clan into a powerful political and military force. A period of unprecedented disruption, fighting and suffering among the chiefdoms followed. People were dispersed and populations decimated through fighting and starvation. Shaka was assassinated in 1828 but many of his policies continued under Dingane. The Zulu chiefdom maintained its powerful position until 1879, when it was defeated by the British Imperial Forces.

The Voortrekkers split into several small groupings throughout the trek, eventually establishing themselves in the two separate republics of the Orange Free State and Transvaal.

The discovery of diamonds in 1867 around Kimberley, and gold on the Witwatersrand in 1886 saw the country's interior transformed. People from all over the world flocked to these regions in search of wealth.

Between 1899–1902 the republics of Transvaal and the Orange Free State were at war with Britain. The war ended with the signing of the Peace Treaty at Vereeniging.

In 1910 the nation became the Union of South Africa. The country was divided into four provinces: Transvaal, Orange Free State, Natal and the Cape Province.

In 1948 the Nationalist Party came to power and introduced its policy of Apartheid, a system of segregation and discrimination on the grounds of race, that was to be in place for over 40 years.

In 1961 South Africa became a Republic, outside the British Commonwealth.

In 1990 Nelson Mandela, the country's foremost African leader, was released from prison, and in April 1994 the country held its first democratic elections in which the whole nation could participate. Nelson Mandela became the first black president of South Africa. During 1994 the land was restructured into nine provinces: Northern Province, North West, Gauteng, Mpumalanga, Northern Cape, Free State, KwaZulu-Natal, Western Cape and Eastern Cape.

Population

Almost 75% of the nation's people are black; the white population accounts for about 13%; and people of Asian and mixed descent 11,2%.

Social and Cultural Profile

It was the world-renowned figure, emeritus Archbishop Desmond Tutu who first referred to South Africa as a rainbow nation of people. The interplay of the richness of cultural and religious diversity gives South Africa its unique character. Each province is an exciting tourist destination in its own right.

Apart from the expected number of museums and historic sites dotted throughout the country, for the benefit of local and foreign tourists there are also cultural villages to be visited in at least seven of the nine provinces. Here one can partake of the traditional way of life of various groups of indigenous people. It is exchanges such as these that increase social and cultural awareness.

▷ *Examples of Ndebele mural art*

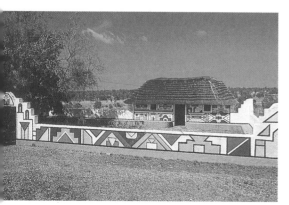

Art

South Africa's association with art dates back to the time of the San rock paintings of animals, hunting scenes, dances and rituals. Other popular art forms that have been practised for centuries include beadwork, woodcarving, basketry and pottery.

The European influence was brought to South African art by early explorers such as Thomas Baines, Fredrick l'Ons and Thomas Bowler. The South African artist Jacob Pierneef is well known for his beautiful paintings depicting typical South African scenery. Other well-known South African artists include Jane Alexander, William Kentridge, Penny Siopis, George Pemba, Walter Battiss, John Muafangelo, Vladimir Tretchikoff, Tinus De Jongh, Gabriel De Jongh, Maggie Laubser, Irma Stern and Gregoire Boonzaaier.

The works of the famous Dutch sculptor, Anton van Wouw, who came to the country in 1890, has also greatly influenced many South African sculptors. The notable work of Anton Anreith can be seen in such fine examples as the famous carved pulpit of the Groote Kerk in Cape Town and the many carvings in the Strand Street Lutheran Church (1776).

Performing Arts

South Africa has an immense wealth of indigenous theatre, which has gained international recognition as many of its artists have performed outside the country. Events such as the Grahamstown Festival have helped expose the nation's talent to the international market. South African music has become popular throughout the world with such internationally recognised artists as Ladysmith Black Mambazo, Mango Groove, Johnny Clegg and Savuka, Miriam Makeba, Leta Mbule,

Hugh Masikela and Kaifas Seminya. The successful team of David Kramer and Taliep Petersen has earned high praise for musical productions such as *District Six* and *Kat and the Kings*, both of which have toured overseas. In 1999, *Kat and the Kings* took London's West End by storm and scooped the coveted Olivier Award for Best New Musical as well as the Best Actor Award for the entire cast! *Sarafina* and *Ipi Ntombi* are other fine stage musicals in a local setting, which also achieved overseas acclaim.

Aubrey Sekhabi, 1998 winner of the country's most prestigious theatre prize, the Standard Bank Young Artist Award, observes that local theatre is "going through a laboratory phase ... so that we can come out at unique ways to tell our stories ...". Multi-talented artists include Gcina Mhlophe (actor, playwright, director), Sello Maake KaNaube and Leleti Khumalo.

Jazz is very popular with a broad spectrum of South African people and can be heard in many of the country's nightclubs and shebeens. The famous jazz pianist and composer Abdullah Ibrahim hails from Manenburg in the Cape. He is also known as Dollar Brand.

Literature

Several well-known writers have portrayed life in Africa to the outside world. Titles that come to mind are *The Suit* by Can Themba, *The Prophetess* by Njabulo Ndebele, *The Collected Works of Herman Charles Bosman, Marabi Dance* by Modikwe Dikobi, *The Story of an African Farm* by Olive Schreiner and *Jock of the Bushveld* by Percy Fitzpatrick. There are countless works by established writers such as Alan Paton, Nadine Gordimer (winner of the Nobel Prize for literature in 1991), Wilbur Smith, Breyten Breytenbach, Etienne Le Roux, André P. Brink, J.M. Coetzee (two-time winner of the Booker Prize) and Peter Abrahams. Although they also write in English and Afrikaans, leading the field of writers in the major languages of isiXhosa, seSotho and isiZulu are Ezekiel Mphahlele, Thomas Mofolo, B.W. Vilakazi, Alex La Guma, J.R. Jolobe and Bloke Modisane.

South Africa has produced poets of the stature of Roy Campbell, F.T. Prince, Roy McNab, Sipho Sepamla and Mongane Wally Serote. In 1973 The Ingrid Jonker Prize for poetry was awarded to Wally Serote and in 1983 he won the Ad. Donker Prize for his outstanding contribution to southern Africa literature during the 1970s. Numbered among established Afrikaans poets are N.P. van Wyk Louw, Uys Krige, Elisabeth Eybers, Breyten Breytenbach and D.J. Opperman who is also a dramatist and respected critic.

Language

Various languages are spoken by South Africa's black population, with the notable exception of the Khoisan. Other tongues introduced into the country by peoples from other lands include English, Afrikaans (developed from Cape Dutch), and Indian dialects of Tamil, Urdu, Hindi and Gujarati. In addition, most Continental languages are heard among the country's large immigrant population.

Religion

Religion plays an important role in the lives of the majority of South Africans and a large percentage of the nation attends church or other places of worship on a regular basis. The constitution guarantees freedom of religion to all citizens and many different beliefs are practised throughout the country. The main religions include Christianity, Islam, Judaism, Hinduism, Buddhism and Indigenous Beliefs.

The African Independent Churches (AIC) consists of many indigenous Christian churches. The AIC was established because of disagreements with certain teachings of Christian missionaries. Some of the followers of the AIC mix Christian religion with traditional African ancestor worship. The largest of the AIC churches is the Zionist Christian Church, whose headquarters is in Moria, near Pietersburg.

Cuisine

South African cuisine is as diverse as its people! The large farming sector provides a variety of animal and vegetable produce, and a wide range of excellent wines, beer and brandy is available as an accompaniment for any relaxed social occasion or fine dining. Specialities of beef, lamb or seafood depend on the region. European, Malay, Indian and African influences are seen in a variety of typical dishes which include bobotie (a curried mince dish), several other forms of curry, bredies (meat, tomato or vegetable stew or a combination of these), sosaties (kebabs), *boerewors* (sausage) and biltong (dried meat). A favourite way of entertaining is the *braai* (barbecue) at which *stywepap* (a thick mealie-meal/maize porridge) is often served as a side dish. Traditional African cooking comprises mainly meat and chicken dishes, mealie-meal porridge, cooked vegetables including spinach (*imifino*), samp (coarsely ground maize) and beans.

Shopping

Popular buys among visitors to South Africa include diamonds, gold jewellery, leather goods, wine, African artefacts and curios.

Festivals and Events

Major events held each year include the Cape Minstrels' Carnival in Cape Town on 2 January, the Argus/Pick 'n Pay Cycle Tour (also in Cape Town) in March, the Comrades Marathon between Pietermaritzburg and Durban during June, and the Standard Bank National Arts Festival held in July in Grahamstown.

Sport and Leisure Facilities

The country is known for its love of sport and its excellent climate allows for countless possibilities for the sporting enthusiast.

Adventure sports are fast becoming a big tourist attraction within South Africa and include white water rafting on the Tugela and Orange Rivers, horse riding safaris, scuba diving, surfing, paragliding and mountain biking. Less energetic activities include golf, whale watching and visits to the spectacular display of wild flowers in Namaqualand, as well as fishing in the country's many dams and rivers.

Spectator sports include events such as road running, boxing and the Million Dollar Golf Challenge, the Comrades Marathon, the Duzi Canoe Marathon, the Gunston 500 surfing championship, the Rothmans July Handicap and Gold Cup horse races, as well as international matches of rugby, cricket and soccer.

Conservation and Eco-Tourism

Eco-tourism is fast becoming an important sector of the market, targeting people who wish to experience the natural environment and cultural heritage of an area without causing a negative impact on the region. South Africa still has large pristine areas of natural beauty, which make it an ideal eco-tourism destination.

NORTHERN PROVINCE

Facts at a Glance

Capital	Pietersburg
Size	123 910 sq km
Population	4,9m
Average Temperature	Summer 17°C min/28°C max
– Pietersburg	Winter 5°C min/20°C max
Main Languages	seSotho, xiTsonga (Shangaan), English, Afrikaans

Geographical Outline

Northern Province shares international borders with Botswana and Zimbabwe to the north and Mozambique to the east. Within South Africa, it borders North West Province to the south-west, Gauteng to the south and Mpumalanga to the south-east.

The landscape of the province is one of bushveld, highveld savannah and subtropical forest. Further north mopani and baobab trees dot the landscape.

The province has several important rivers – Limpopo, Olifants, Great Letaba, Crocodile – and the Mokolo and Tzaneen dams are the main water storage facilities. Mountains include the Soutpansberg, Drakensberg, Strydpoortberge and the Waterberg ranges.

Introduction

The Region

Northern Province is a region of great beauty and natural diversity complemented by a rich historical and cultural heritage. It has much to offer the would-be tourist, including numerous wildlife parks and nature reserves, a wealth of hot spring resorts, ancient forests and beautiful mountain scenery.

The Economy

Mining and agriculture are important sectors of the economy. The province has an abundance of mineral resources including iron ore, chromium, coal, diamonds, phosphate and copper. The main agricultural products include subtropical fruit, tea, coffee, cotton, tobacco, maize and wheat. Other significant economic sectors are livestock farming and forestry.

The Importance of Tourism

Tourism is fairly underdeveloped in the region although there is great potential. Consideration is being given to linking the Kruger National Park with the wildlife parks of Mozambique. The park lies along the entire eastern section of the province adjoining the Mozambique border.

Climate

The Tropic of Capricorn runs through Northern Province and temperatures can become extremely high, especially in the subtropical eastern Lowveld region where summer temperatures can reach as high as 45°C with frequent afternoon thunderstorms. Winter days are warm and sunny with cold mornings and nights on the Highveld plateau.

Transportation and Accessibility

Road

The NI highway bisects the province joining Gauteng with Pietersburg, Louis Trichardt and Messina before it reaches the Zimbabwean border. The N11 crosses the province from the Botswana border in the west through to Mpumalanga in the east. An efficient network of secondary roads connects all the main centres throughout the province.

Border crossings into Botswana are at Stockpoort, Parr's Halt, Martin's Drift, Groblersbrug, (between 08:00–18:00), Zanzibar, Platjan, Pontdrif (between 08:00–16:00), and at Beit Bridge into Zimbabwe (between 05:30–22:30).

Coaches operate daily between Johannesburg and Pietersburg and there are several regional bus services operating within the province.

Air

Flights operate between Johannesburg and Pietersburg's Gateway International Airport, Hoedspruit and Phalaborwa.

Rail

Mainline trains connect Johannesburg with Messina via Pretoria, Pietersburg and Louis Trichardt.

Accommodation

The province has several first class hotels and country lodges, such as the Magoebaskloof Hotel in Magoebaskloof and the Coach House Country Hotel in

Tzaneen. There are also numerous resorts, chalets, cottages, guesthouses and bed and breakfast establishments, as well as well-equipped caravan and camp sites scattered throughout the province. Visitors to game lodges experience the varied landscape and vegetation whilst enjoying the abundance of animal and bird life.

Historic Highlights

Rock artwork found throughout the province documents the survival techniques of the San who inhabited the region during the Later Stone Age period.

Successive waves of people have migrated from the north into the region during the past 2 000 years.

During the 1840s the Voortrekkers arrived in the area, playing a significant role in its history. Many of the province's main centres, such as Louis Trichardt and Pietersburg, are named after Voortrekker leaders.

Population

The main groups who have settled within the borders of Northern Province include the Tswana, Pedi, Ndebele, Tsonga (Shangaan), Venda, Lemba, Lobedu, and others who are mainly of Voortrekker descent.

Social and Cultural Profile

Most of the people live in small towns and rural communities. Music and dance are an integral part of the way of life of several communities. The well-known slow and rhythmic python dance is performed by young Venda girls. A love of design and colour is particularly associated with the Ndebele who are responsible for vibrant mural art.

The region has been immortalised by several European and South African writers of European origin. John Buchan, who resided in the Magoebaskloof district, centered his novel *Prester John* on the area, and the novel *She*, by Rider Haggard, is believed to be based on the Rain Queen Modjadji.

Eugene Marais and Gerhard Moerdyk are other well-known authors from this part of South Africa.

Sport and Leisure Facilities

The province has many venues for sport lovers and adventure seekers. Hiking, climbing, 4 x 4 driving, mountain biking and horse riding trails are popular throughout the region. Canoe excursions operate on the Limpopo River and fishing is popular here and in the Magoebaskloof region. More leisurely pastimes such as golf, tennis and bowls are all well catered for and the many mineral springs throughout the region provide a perfect way to relax.

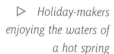
▷ Holiday-makers enjoying the waters of a hot spring

Hiking

There are numerous hiking trails to be found throughout the province. The Rooikat Trail, an 11km, 5-hour circular hiking trail, passes through the forest near Tzaneen, and can be completed in a morning, starting and ending at the New Agatha Forest Station some 18km south-west of Tzaneen. The Soutpansberg Hiking Trail splits into different sections of varying lengths, and the Magoebaskloof Hiking Trail traverses the beautiful Magoebaskloof valley. Other popular trails include the Wolkberg Wilderness Area, several trails around the Ellisras area, and the Mabudashango Trail, a 54km circular route which starts at the Vhulanda (Thathe Vondo) Forest Station, passing through indigenous forest and the sacred Lake Fundudzi.

Game Hunting

The province has several hunting farms and lodges. Hunting is strictly controlled and part of the revenue gained from this exploit is reinvested into conservation.

Conservation and Eco-Tourism

Numerous centres for endangered animals exist throughout the province. These are the game breeding centre close to Potgietersrus, which forms part of the National Zoological Gardens of Pretoria; Mossie Mostert's Game Farm, where innovative breeding programmes have assisted in the protection of the White Lions of Timbavati; and the Kapama Cheetah Centre at Hoedspruit which is involved in a unique cheetah breeding project. In addition, the area is home to the Moholoholo Bird Rehabilitation Centre near Hoedspruit, and the Moletzie Bird Sanctuary close to Pietersburg which is involved in the protection of the rare Cape Vulture.

Various areas of the province have been set aside to protect the region's large variety of indigenous flora. These include the Wolkberg Wilderness Area, the Cycad Forests near Duiwelskloof, the Soutpansberg mountain range and the Messina Nature Reserve.

Wildlife Parks and Nature Reserves

Kruger National Park

Although the Kruger National Park north of the Olifants River falls within Northern Province, the entire park is covered in the chapter on Mpumalanga. However, many of the park's northern gates are easily accessed by travelling through Northern Province.

Pietersburg Game Reserve

The 3 000ha Pietersburg Game Reserve is well stocked with a variety of game and has an abundance of bird life. There is an 18km circular walk known as the Rhino Trail that takes you through the reserve.

Hans Merensky Nature Reserve

Situated some 50km to the west of the Kruger National Park border, the Hans Merensky Nature Reserve covers an area of some 5 200 hectares of bushveld along the Great Letaba River. The reserve has an abundance of game, over 300 species of bushveld birds and is an important breeding area for the sable antelope. There are four marked walking trails within the reserve which range from the 1,2km Mopane Interpretive Trail to the three-day Giraffe Hiking Trail. The nearby Aventura Eiland Resort, built on a mineral spring on the banks of the Great Letaba River, provides accommodation, entertainment and sport facilities.

Modjadji Nature Reserve

The Modjadji Nature Reserve is situated 29km north-east of Duiwelskloof. The 305ha reserve protects an ancient forest of cycads and is home to the Lobedu people's hereditary ruler, the Rain Queen Modjadji. The Rain Queen is thought to have descended from a 16th century Karanga princess who fled across the Limpopo River from Zimbabwe and found refuge in the cycad forest. Believed to possess rain magic, the Rain Queen still plays an important role in the region. Various short walking trails through the reserve pass by Modjadji's sacred cycad forest. The reserve has a picnic and braai (barbecue) area, an information centre, kiosk and curio shop.

Wolkberg Wilderness Area

The 22 000ha wilderness area was proclaimed in 1977 and is a popular venue for experienced hikers. The terrain is rugged and there are no set routes, overnight huts for hikers or facilities for visitors.

Ben Levin Nature Reserve

Situated some 12km south-east of Louis Trichardt, the 2 500ha Ben Levin Nature Reserve is home to over 50 different mammal species and 230 species of bird. Visitors may explore its mixed bushveld terrain on foot – by way of the four marked circular trails which range from four to eight kilometres in length – or drive through the 40-kilometre network of gravel roads. Accommodation is available in thatched huts or hired tents and there is also a campsite for tents.

Messina Nature Reserve

Situated in the far northern part of the province, the Messina Nature Reserve covers an area of some 4 900ha and boasts over 12 000 specimens of baobab as well as mopane, white seringa, bushwillow, shepherd's tree and corkwood. The

reserve is also home to the nyala, kudu, sable antelope, leopard, Sharpe's grysbok and giraffe as well as some 187 different species of bird. There is a 23km circular drive that takes you through the reserve and hiking trails may be arranged through the officer-in-charge.

▷ *A Baobab tree*

Nwanedi National Park

Located approximately 65km from Thohoyandou, Nwanedi National Park is known for its popular angling sites at the Nwanedi and Luphephe dams. Game found within the park includes white rhino, eland, kudu and giraffe.

Other places of interest are the D'Nyala Nature Reserve near Ellisras, the Marakele National Park near Thabazimbi, the Ndlazama Game Reserve at Letsitele near Tzaneen, and the Langjan Nature Reserve near Louis Trichardt, which is a sanctuary for South Africa's remaining gemsbok.

Tourist Attractions

Northern Region

The Soutpansberg

The Soutpansberg mountain range stretches across the northern reaches of Northern Province. It is an area of beauty, myths and legends as well as a haven for a large variety of fauna, flora and bird species. Evidence of its former inhabitants can be found in the ancient ruins, archaeological sites and rock engravings found throughout the region.

Venda

Venda is situated in the north-eastern part of the province and is an area of great natural beauty, filled with streams and waterfalls and indigenous woodland. The culture of the Venda people is steeped in legends and superstition and many areas are considered sacred. Well-known traditional handicrafts, especially pottery and woodcarvings, are of a high standard and can be found at various craft centres.

The choice of accommodation includes hotels and lodges as well as self-catering units. Sun International's luxury hotel, the Venda Sun, offers its visitors a casino and sport and conference facilities.

Thathe Vondo Forest

The magnificent Thathe Vondo Forest is situated between Thohoyandou and Makhado. Places of interest within the forest include Lake Fundudzi, the Sacred Forest, Mahovhohovho Falls, Mukumbani Dam and the Thathe Tea Estates.

Tshipise Spa and Honnet Nature Reserve

Situated in the bushveld to the north of Louis Trichardt are the Aventura Tshipise Spa Resort and Honnet Nature Reserve. The resort is a large, well-equipped complex that was developed on the site of two hot mineral springs. The nearby Honnet Nature Reserve, covering an area of some 2 200ha of mopane and other indigenous trees, is home to a variety of game and several species of bird. Apart from horse riding trails, there is a two-day circular hiking trail, known as the Baobab Trail. Accommodation is in self-catering rondavels or at the campsite.

Central Region

Pietersburg

The city of Pietersburg has several fascinating historical sites and tourist attractions. Its elevated position of 1 312m above sea level ensures a temperate climate. There are excellent sport facilities for golf, tennis and swimming. Places of interest include the Bakoni Malapa Northern Sotho Open-air Museum depicting the traditional and modern-day culture and lifestyle of the Bakoni people; the Pietersburg Museum, which houses exhibits detailing the history of the city; the Hugh Exton Photographic Museum that captures the first 50 years of the town's history; the Moletzie Bird Sanctuary, and the Pietersburg Game Reserve.

Tourism Destinations Southern Africa

Tzaneen

Situated in the Lowveld, Tzaneen has several places worth visiting in close proximity to the town as well as within the town itself. Of particular interest are the Tzaneen Museum with its exhibits of ethnological artefacts; the New Agatha Forest Station, once a staging post of the Zeederberg Coach Company; and the Sapekoe Tea Estate.

Magoebaskloof Pass

The beautiful Magoebaskloof Pass links the Highveld town of Haenertsburg to Tzaneen in the Lowveld. The 25km pass drops dramatically over the Drakensberg Escarpment, providing some spectacular viewing as the road passes through indigenous forest, pine plantations and mountain slopes. Several fine hotels and self-catering accommodation are to be found in the vicinity.

Debengeni Falls

Debengeni is an enchantingly beautiful site half hidden in the forests of the Magoebaskloof. The waters of the Ramadipa River cascade some 80m down into a natural basin below. The site has a beautiful picnic and braai area at the foot of the falls from where several short walks lead into the De Hoek State Forest.

Ebenezer Dam

The Ebenezer Dam is situated close to Haenertsburg, some 35km west of Tzaneen. The dam is fed by the Letaba River and is surrounded by beautiful scenery. The bilharzia-free waters make it a favourite venue for water sport enthusiasts and anglers alike.

Western Region

Waterberg

The Waterberg region of the province has a wealth of indigenous flora and fauna as well as superb scenery. It is fast becoming a popular venue for nature lovers and adventure sport enthusiasts where outdoor activities can be enjoyed in the many game and nature reserves and on working farms. On offer are activities such as hiking, guided bush walks, game drives, bird watching, fishing, hunting, horse riding safaris and mountain bike trails.

Lapalala Wilderness

Lapalala is a 25 000ha wilderness sanctuary situated in the Waterberg mountains some three and a half hours from Johannesburg. The reserve's main concern is the conservation and breeding of endangered species. It is a quiet, malaria-free area of mixed and sour bushveld. Visitors must explore the region on foot, as driving is not permitted in the reserve. Game found within the sanctuary includes white and black rhino, sable and roan antelope, hippos, giraffe and over 280 different species of bird. The reserve also has Stone Age sites, Iron-Age ruins and San rock paintings. Accommodation is available at self-catering camps, as well as at the Rhino Camp and Kolobe Lodge.

Warmbaths Spa

The Warmbaths Spa and Aventura Resort is situated about 100km north of Pretoria and is a popular day and weekend retreat for the people of Gauteng. The complex has several hot and cold pools as well as a 'supertube' and wave pool. There are numerous self-catering chalets, hotels, camp and caravan parks located within the area.

Eastern Region

Phalaborwa

It is believed that the Nguni people mined copper and iron centuries ago in the region between the Olifants and Letaba rivers. Today the town of Phalaborwa is one of South Africa's principal mining centres. There are three main roads connecting Phalaborwa with Gauteng, and daily flights operate from Johannesburg. The town is a short distance from the Kruger National Park and offers night drives into the park. The Foskor Museum follows the town's mining history and that of the people who have settled within the region.

Historic Sites

Numerous historic sites and national monuments are to be found within Northern Province, details of which can be obtained from the tourist information offices. Important sites include the Makapansgat Caves, near Potgietersrus, where evidence of prehistoric human habitation has been found; the Dzata Ruins, site of the Venda kings' royal village dating back to the 1400s; and the Eersteling Gold Mine where the first gold was mined and smelted in the Transvaal in 1871.

Cultural Villages

Bakoni Malapa Museum

Situated some nine kilometres from Pietersburg, the Bakoni Malapa Museum offers its visitors an insight into the lifestyles of the Bakoni of Matala, a sub-group of Northern Sotho people. Skilled craftsmen and craftswomen live in and maintain the museum providing visitors with an opportunity to buy some of their traditional handicrafts. There is a hiking trail behind the museum, which offers fine views of the kraal layout.

Other cultural villages include the Nyani Tribal Village at Klaserie; the Shangaan and Pedi villages near Tzaneen; and the Tshakuma Village near Levubu where the work of traditional VhaVenda sculptors and craftsmen can be seen.

Activity

Your client is staying for seven days at the 5-star Coach House Hotel in Tzaneen. Draw up a list of possible day trips available within the region, suggesting sport activities as well as sightseeing options.

NORTH WEST PROVINCE

Facts at a Glance

Capital	Mmabatho
Size	116 320 sq km
Population	3,4m
Average Temperature – Mmabatho	Summer min 22°C/max 34°C Winter min 2°C/max 18°C
Main Languages	isiXhosa, seTswana, seSotho, Afrikaans, English

Geographical Outline

North West Province borders on Gauteng to the east, the Northern Province to the north-east, Free State to the south-east, Northern Cape to the south-west and Botswana to the north-west.

Its terrain varies from rugged bushveld and semi-arid scrub in the west to large expanses of rich fertile soil in the southern and eastern regions.

The Magaliesberg mountain range runs westwards through the province for some 120km from the outskirts of Pretoria to the town of Rustenburg. Important rivers and dams in the region include the Vaal, Harts and Mooi rivers and the Hartbeespoort, Bloemhof and Wentzel dams.

Introduction

The Region

The province's close proximity to Johannesburg and Pretoria make it an ideal short-stay venue for travellers. Its major tourist attractions are the Sun City complex, the adjacent Pilanesburg National Park, Hartbeespoort Dam and the Vaal River resorts.

The Economy

The main industries of the region are agriculture and mining.

Two of the world's largest platinum mines are to be found in Rustenburg and gold and platinum are mined in Klerksdorp. Agriculture plays an important role in the economy of the province producing crops such as maize, citrus and tobacco.

The Importance of Tourism

Evidence of the province's positive approach to tourism is already clearly manifested in the area in and around Sun City and the Hartbeespoort Dam, where there is an abundance of bed and breakfast establishments, restaurants and art and craft markets. The more remote rural towns are fast becoming aware of the benefits of tourism and are very much involved in the promotion of their own tourist attractions.

Climate

North West Province has clear sunny days for most of the year. It is a summer rainfall area when afternoon thunderstorms often occur. Summers tend to be very hot during the day and warm at night. Winter is generally warm during the day and cold at night.

Transportation and Accessibility

Road

The region can be easily accessed from both Johannesburg and Pretoria and has an efficient road network. The N4 traverses the northern part of the province towards the Botswana border; the N14 covers the central area and continues to Northern Cape; and the N12 takes the southerly route towards Christiana. Numerous tarred subsidiary roads connect the various towns throughout the region.

A daily inter-city bus service operates from Johannesburg to Mafikeng and Potchefstroom and car hire facilities are available at Sun City.

Air

Return flights are scheduled from Johannesburg to Mmabatho and Sun City.

Rail

There is a train service which operates between Johannesburg and Mafikeng (Mmabatho).

Accommodation

Accommodation is plentiful throughout the province. There are several three- and four-star hotels and resorts, first class game lodges, conference venues, bed and breakfast and guest farm accommodation, as well as camp and caravan sites.

Historic Highlights

During the early part of the 19th century, Mzilikazi and his Matabele followers dominated the region until the 1830s when they were driven across the Limpopo River (into present-day Zimbabwe) by white settlers.

Diamonds were discovered around Lichtenburg during the 1870s.

In 1885 the British established the British Bechuanaland Protectorate and chose Mafeking (original spelling) as its capital. The name Mafikeng (as it is now correctly written) means 'place of stones'. It is particularly remembered in connection with the 280-day siege it underwent during the Anglo–Boer War of 1899.

In 1977 several areas within the province fell under the independent homeland of Bophuthatswana, with Mmabatho as its capital.

Population

The inhabitants of the province are mainly of Tswana and Voortrekker descent.

Social and Cultural Profile

North West has a rich cultural heritage and numerous visual displays of the traditional way of life are found within the province. Several cultural villages exist, art and craft markets produce local handicrafts and household wares, cultural festivals are held throughout the year and the region has many singing and dancing groups.

The Afrikaans culture is felt throughout the province in its atmospheric rural towns and communities. The region has been immortalised by the well-known South African writer, Herman Charles Bosman, in works such as *Mafeking Road* and *Willem Prinsloo's Peach Brandy*, which are set in the bushveld region of Groot Marico.

Sport and Leisure Facilities

The province has a wealth of excellent sport and leisure facilities. The Sun City resort offers many sport and leisure options. Yachting, water-skiing and windsurfing facilities are provided at the Bloemhof Dam on the Vaal River, the Hartbeespoort Dam and Wentzel Dam near Schweizer-Reneke. Other popular pastimes well catered for include river rafting, canoeing, fishing, mountain climbing, mountain biking, abseiling, hang-and paragliding, tennis and golf.

Hiking

The region has numerous hiking trails. Popular among them are the Enzelberg and Langkloof trails in the Marico Valley; the Leon Taljaard and Vryburg walks in the Bophirima region; the Summit, Boat and Paddle, Mooirivier, Pioneers' Route Inner City and Rooihuis trails, as well as the Thabela Thabeng hiking trails in the Potchefstroom region. In addition, there are the Makwassierante Conservation Area hiking trails close to Wolmaransstad.

Horse Trails

Horse trails have become a popular pastime and are available at the Rhino Rock Horse Trail and Riding School near Klerksdorp, and the Roberts Farm Horse Trails near Rustenburg.

Hot-Air Ballooning

Hot-air balloons floating across blue skies are a common sight in North West Province. Champagne breakfast flights over the Magaliesberg can be booked through Bill Harrops Balloon Safaris, or reservations can be made at Sun City for flights over the Pilanesburg National Park.

Gambling and Entertainment

Apart from the Sun City complex, the province offers several other gambling and entertainment venues including the Carousel Entertainment complex, the Morula Sun Leisure Resort, the Mmabatho Sun, and the Taung Sun.

Conservation and Eco-Tourism

North West Province has a deep commitment to the conservation of the region. Located within its borders are two centres for endangered species. The Lichtenburg Game-Breeding Centre, which forms part of the National Zoological Gardens, breeds rare and endangered species of wildlife, including the pygmy hippo and the scimitar-horned oryx. De Wildt Cheetah Research Centre, situated near Brits, specialises in the breeding and study of cheetah, king cheetah, wild dogs, brown hyena, suni and blue duiker.

Many of the region's rural towns are developing their own unique style of eco-tourism. The Groot Marico region boasts more than five veld types, 200 different indigenous tree species and more than 430 bird species. The town itself offers custom-made and special interest excursions, such as *mampoer* (home-made brandy) tours and guided weekend hikes. Visitors are able to experience rural life by staying in one of the many farmhouses in the region. Camping and caravan facilities are available on the banks of the Marico River and the Marico Bushveld Dam.

The establishment of the Madikwe Game Reserve is another example of how tourism is assisting the people of the region. The creation of this game park in an economically depressed part of the province was found to be a better option than agriculture or cattle farming. It has provided improved employment opportunities and money-earning potential, which in turn benefit the surrounding communities.

Wildlife Parks and Nature Reserves

Pilanesburg National Park

This park is arguably the region's premier reserve. It covers some 55 000ha of an extinct volcano, measuring some 27km in diameter. The scenic landscape is dominated by the beauty of a large central lake surrounded by open plains of acacia, savannah and grassland, wooded valleys and deep ravines. Stone and Iron Age sites are found throughout the park. In 1979 animals were introduced into the park and during 1999 wild dogs were added to the other 89 different species of mammal that include the endangered white and black rhino, buffalo, lion, leopard, cheetah, elephant, and over 300 different bird species.

The park has almost 200 kilometres of good roads and offers self-driven tours or professionally guided drives, guided night-drives, wilderness trails and a self-driven geology trail. It is even possible to enjoy a bird's eye view from a hot-air balloon.

Accommodation within the park includes several first class resorts offering tent or cabin accommodation as well as caravan parks and campsites. There are also picnic and braai facilities.

Madikwe Game Reserve

The Madikwe Game Reserve, situated on the province's northern border with Botswana, covers an area of some 75 000ha and is located within a malaria-free region of the country. The park is home to white rhino and the rare black rhino, buffalo, elephant, lion, leopard and cheetah, as well as several different species of antelope.

The Tau Game Lodge, located within the Madikwe Reserve, donates a percentage of its revenue to wild dog and predator monitoring in the reserve. Tau consists of some 30 air-conditioned chalets overlooking a waterhole. It also offers conference facilities.

Borakalalo Nature Reserve

Situated 60km north of Brits, the Borakalalo Nature Reserve covers an area of 14 000ha and offers some 100km of gravel roads for game viewing as well as self-guided walks and wilderness trails. The vegetation consists mainly of woodland and riverine forest along the Moretele River. There are some 35 species of mammal, including white rhino, and 350 different bird species. The Klipvoor Dam within the park, is a popular fishing spot. Safari tent accommodation is offered at the Phudufudu and Moretele Camps and there are several campsites located around the Pitjane Camp.

Rustenburg Nature Reserve

The reserve is located a few kilometres south-west of the town of Rustenburg and offers game viewing and several self-guided hiking trails. Day-visitor facilities exist for picnicking, braaiing (barbecuing), walking, game and bird viewing. Overnight camping and hiking facilities are available.

Tourist Attractions

Sun City and the Lost City Complex

The internationally renowned Sun City complex is North West's biggest tourist attraction and is popular with both foreign and domestic guests.

The complex is set in beautifully landscaped grounds. There are four hotels, a casino, an entertainment centre, a 6 000-seater 'superbowl', an extravaganza theatre, conference facilities, restaurants, shops, cinemas and discos. Other attractions are a walk-in aviary, swimming pools, a fully equipped health spa and numerous sport and leisure facilities. The Million Dollar Challenge is held annually on its famous golf course.

▷ *The Lost City complex*

The Sun City Hotel

The Sun City Hotel is set in beautifully manicured lawns. It has several fine restaurants, a large swimming pool and is home to the Casino and Extravaganza Theatre.

The Cabanas

The Cabanas is a family-orientated hotel with rooms that open onto the lawns and Waterworld. It has its own swimming pool, pool bar, and buffet terrace.

The Cascades

This is a luxury five-star hotel set in tropically landscaped grounds full of waterfalls, streams and pools, which are home to swans, flamingos and other exotic birds. The hotel foyer, restaurants and bars open onto a lake, waterfalls and a shady grotto, giving the hotel a relaxed atmosphere.

The Palace of the Lost City

The luxurious Palace of the Lost City Hotel is surrounded by 25ha of jungle and was designed to resemble a recently discovered ancient city. The complex includes the Valley of Waves – a huge artificial wave pool which laps onto a white-sand beach.

▷ *Palace of the Lost City*

Sport facilities available at the resort include tennis, squash, bowls, tenpin bowling, swimming and horse riding. There is also a health club with sauna, a gymnasium and aerated spa and two golf courses. Water sports such as water-skiing, windsurfing, jet-skiing and parasailing are available at the extensive lake situated below the Cabanas hotel.

Various tourist attractions have been established close to the Sun City and Lost City complex. The Kwena Gardens Crocodile Paradise is located at the entrance to Sun City; the Lion Park, situated next to Sundown Ranch, is a short distance from the complex; and the African Game and Art Centre, which offers ostrich rides, restaurants and conference facilities, is at Boshoek.

Hartbeespoort Dam

Situated to the south of the Magaliesberg mountain range, Hartbeespoort Dam is a popular venue for day and weekend visitors from nearby Gauteng. The region has numerous hiking trails and excellent facilities for water sport enthusiasts, which include yachting, water-skiing and windsurfing.

Some of the main tourist attractions within the area are the Snake and Animal Park, the Hartbeespoort Cableway, Tan' Malie se Winkel (Aunt Malie's Shop) and the Makalani Bird Sanctuary. An unusual lunchtime option, by way of floating across the dam whilst enjoying lunch, is offered by African Water Safaris.

There are numerous bed and breakfast, chalet and camping facilities available in the area.

Vaal River

The Vaal River forms the province's southern border with Free State and is a favourite recreational haunt for the people of Gauteng. The region has numerous leisure resorts and nature reserves and provides facilities for a variety of sport activities. The Bloemhof Dam and Nature Reserve and the towns of Bloemhof and Christiana are established tourist attractions.

Historic Sites

Taung Skull Heritage Site

The Taung Skull Heritage Site marks the spot where the Taung child skull was discovered in 1924.

Vredefort Dome

The Vredefort Dome was created when a meteorite crashed into the earth some 2 000 million years ago.

Boekenhoutfontein

Boekenhoutfontein, the former homestead of Paul Kruger is situated close to the town of Rustenburg. Parts of the original homestead have been restored and transformed into a museum that is open to the public.

Battlefields

Many famous battle sites are to be found within the area, including the site of the 280-day Siege of Mafeking.

San Rock Art

San rock art can be viewed at Stowlands, 6km out of Christiana; on the farm Bosworth, near to Klerksdorp; and 2km north-east of the town of Schweizer-Reneke on the Delareyville Road.

Cultural Villages

Rainbow Cultural Village

On offer are tours through a Ndebele village and a San bush residence. There is also an opportunity to sample traditional Afrikaans cuisine at the Boer Farmyard or to be entertained at Sophia's Tavern Shebeen.

Lotlamoreng Dam Cultural Reserve

The reserve, situated close to Mafikeng, is a living museum portraying several different traditional villages.

Kortkloof Tswana Village

Situated close to Groot Marico, visitors are here given a taste of everyday Tswana village life.

Activity

Describe the amenities offered at the Sun City and Lost City resort and in the surrounding area.

Outline the differences between the complex's four hotels, such as grading and style.

What are the benefits of establishing a tourist attraction close to the Sun City complex?

4 GAUTENG

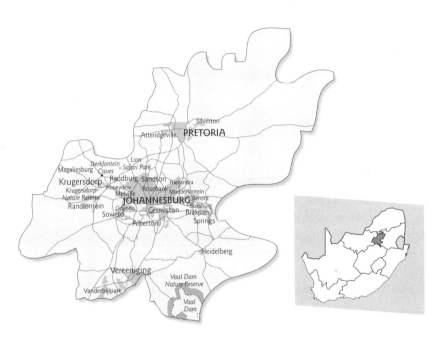

Facts at a Glance

Capital	Johannesburg
Size	17 010 sq km
Population	7,3m
Average Temperature	Summer min 14°C/max 26°C
– Johannesburg	Winter min 4°C/max16°C
Main Languages	Afrikaans, English, seSotho, seTswana, isiZulu

Geographical Outline

Situated entirely on the vast interior plateau known as the Highveld, Gauteng is bordered to the north by Northern Province, to the west by North West Province, to the south by Free State and to the east by Mpumalanga. Important mountains and rivers include the Magaliesberg mountain range, lying to the east of Pretoria, and the Vaal River, which forms its southern boundary with Free State.

Introduction

The Region

Gauteng is the smallest, richest and most dynamic province of South Africa. It is the commercial heart of the nation and has a well-developed communication and transportation infrastructure and a thriving business sector. Important cities within the province include Johannesburg, the capital of the province, Pretoria, the country's administrative capital, and the sprawling expanse of vibrant Soweto. Despite its size and vast areas of urbanisation, the province boasts many open spaces for recreational activities.

The Economy

The Gauteng regional economy is the largest in the country. Its most important sectors include manufacturing, finance, insurance, business services, real estate and mining.

The Importance of Tourism

Although it is not one of the country's main tourism destinations, it has much to offer by way of historical and cultural attractions as well as wide open spaces of scenic beauty.

One of the region's main detractions is the high crime rate associated with areas such as Johannesburg, and it is essential to caution visitors regarding personal safety.

Climate

Gauteng is situated in the summer rainfall area. Summer days are warm to hot, with occasional afternoon thunderstorms. The province's high altitude determines that days rarely become unbearably hot during the summer. While daytime temperatures during the winter months are usually mild and the days are sunny, at night the temperature often drops below zero. Pretoria and the northern part of the province tend to be slightly warmer than Johannesburg.

Transportation and Accessibility

Road

The province has an extensive route network allowing for easy access to most of the country's main tourist attractions. The N1 highway, which runs from Cape Town to the country's northern border, traverses the province; the N4 runs across the northern part of the province from the Botswana to the Mozambique border; the N3 connects Gauteng with Free State and KwaZulu-Natal; the N12 crosses the province from Witbank in Mpumalanga through Klerksdorp in North West Province and on to Northern Cape Province; the N14 runs from Pretoria to Northern Cape via North West Province; and the N17 runs from Germiston to Swaziland via Ermelo in Mpumalanga.

Buses and coaches depart from Johannesburg and Pretoria to all main centres throughout the country. All the major car hire companies have offices in Johannesburg and at Johannesburg International Airport.

Air

Gauteng Province is home to the nation's main airport, Johannesburg International Airport, which is served by most international, regional and domestic carriers. Charter airlines operate from Lanseria, Grand Central and Rand airports in the Johannesburg area and Wonderboom, north of Pretoria.

Rail

There is an extensive network of both mainline and regional trains operating throughout the province. The Blue Train and Rovos Rail depart from Pretoria Station.

Accommodation

Ranging from 5-star hotels and luxury country lodges to guesthouses, bed and breakfast facilities, self-catering units, and camp and caravan sites, accommodation is available to suit all tastes and budgets. Hotel groups include Sun International, Southern Sun, Protea Hotels, Holiday Inn, Karos, Best Western and City Lodge. There are also a large number of conference venues within the province. These include the Aloe Ridge Hotel and Game Reserve, Heia Safari Lodge in the Western Gauteng region, Gallagher Estate, Midrand, the Sinodale Conference Centre, the CSIR Conference Centre in the Pretoria area, and several in the Magaliesberg region.

Historic Highlights

In 1886 gold was discovered on the Witwatersrand changing the history of the region and the entire nation. Gold brought people from all corners of the world to the area.

Population

All of South Africa's main ethnic groups as well as nationalities from all over the world are represented within Gauteng Province.

Social and Cultural Profile

The word Gauteng is a seSotho word meaning 'Place of Gold' and it highlights the foundation upon which the region was built to become what it is today.

The many cultural groups that live and work in and around the cities of the province have contributed, along with the rural communities, to the making of the province's vibrant and unique culture. Most of its city dwellers are dynamic and success-oriented people who work hard and play hard. They enjoy the artistic and cultural aspects of city life and frequent its entertainment venues, restaurants, bars and nightclubs. Leisure time often revolves around participating in or watching the many sport activities the province has to offer.

Sport and Leisure Facilities

The nation's three main spectator sports of rugby, soccer and cricket are well catered for, with rugby stadiums at Ellis Park in Johannesburg and Loftus Versveld in Pretoria; cricket pitches at the Wanderers in Johannesburg and Centurion Park in Pretoria; and soccer venues at the First National Bank Stadium, the Orlando Stadium, the Rand Stadium and Soccer City in Johannesburg. Other facilities include those for tennis at the Standard Bank Indoor Tennis Arena and Ellis Park Tennis Stadium; athletics at the Johannesburg and Ruimsig athletics stadiums; and horse racing at Turffontein, Gosforth Park and Newmarket. In addition, there are numerous superb golf courses and health clubs located within the province, which are well patronised by the people of Gauteng.

Traditional dancing and mine dancing may be seen at several venues, such as Gold Reef City and the Heia Safari Ranch, the Aloe Ridge Hotel and the various cultural villages.

Hiking

There are many interesting walks and hikes in and around the city centres. Information is available at tourist information offices.

Water Sport

Water sport facilities exist on the region's rivers and dams. Power boating, sailing, water- and jet-skiing, river rafting and canoe safaris are catered for at popular sites such as the Vaal River and Vaal Dam.

Gambling and Entertainment

As a result of the change in South Africa's Gambling Act and the awarding of legal casino licences, gambling has become a popular pastime. The Sundrome Casino, just off the N1 close to Roodepoort, and Caesars Gauteng Hotel Casino and Convention Resort at Johannesburg International Airport, are established venues.

▷ *Visitors at a gambling table*

Conservation and Eco-Tourism

The National Zoological Gardens in Pretoria has been involved with conservation work for some time and is participating in several international projects, as well as the management of game breeding centres in North West and Northern provinces.

Wildlife Parks and Nature Reserves

There are several small game reserves located around Gauteng Province, offering visitors with time constraints an opportunity to view Africa's game within close proximity of Johannesburg or Pretoria.

Krugersdorp Nature Reserve

The 1 400ha game reserve offers visitors a chance to view several species of game including lion, rhino, kudu, giraffe and zebra. Accommodation and conference facilities are available at the reserve, as well as two swimming pools, a braai (barbecue) and picnic area and children's playground.

Lion Safari Park

The park is located 30km north of Johannesburg in 200ha of grassland and forest. The lion enclosure consists of six well-fenced camps where various prides live and breed. Facilities for visitors include a restaurant, curio shop, a braai area and a picnic area.

Rhino and Lion Reserve

Situated some 30 minutes drive from central Johannesburg is the Rhino and Lion Nature Reserve. It boasts some 500 head of game including white rhino, lion, hippo, and buffalo. Overnight accommodation is available in fully equipped chalets. Day and night game drives can be arranged in advance and facilities exist for private functions and conferences. For the convenience of day-visitors there is a swimming pool, kiosk and curio shop and a braai area.

Witwatersrand National Botanical Garden

The Witwatersrand National Botanical Garden is made up of a network of eight botanical gardens, herbaria and centres for environmental education and research. The Witpoortjie Waterfall and surrounding rock face is a central feature of the gardens, and the cliff face next to the waterfall is home to a pair of breeding black eagles. The park has a geological trail as well as several short trails that take visitors through its diverse vegetation.

Tourist Attractions

Johannesburg

The city of Johannesburg has much to offer tourists and there are several worthwhile tours available which give an insight into its history and culture. Many beautiful parks, gardens and open spaces enable visitors to enjoy the Highveld scenery. Information about local tour companies and the many tourist attractions of the region is available at tourist information offices and at the reception desks of most hotels.

Popular tours offered from Johannesburg include:

▶ Johannesburg City Tour
▶ Tour of Soweto
▶ Gold Reef City
▶ Cultural Villages
▶ Sun City/Lost City

Countless shopping opportunities exist in upmarket shopping malls such as Sandton City, Rosebank and Eastgate and there are numerous shops, restaurants, bars and bistros to be found in other popular areas such as Melville. The city also has several well-supported flea markets including 'the roof' at Rosebank Mall on Sunday and at Bruma Lake.

Gold Reef City

Located just 8km to the south of central Johannesburg, Gold Reef City is one of the area's most popular tourist destinations. It is easily accessed by road and there are several companies that offer day tours. The complex is built around an authentic gold mine and underground tours are offered. Other interesting exhibits include gold pouring demonstrations and turn-of-the-century mine dwellings. Traditional song and dance, including the stirring gumboot dance, is performed daily.

▷ *The gumboot dance*

▷ *A woman doing a traditional dance*

There are several shops and restaurants dotted throughout the city, as well as a variety of rides at the funfair. Transport is provided by means of train or horse-drawn carriage.

Accommodation is available at the Gold Reef City Hotel where rooms are reproductions of typical turn-of-the-century hotel decor.

▷ *A horse-drawn carriage at Gold Reef City*

Gold Mine Tours

Various tours are available to view other working mines and can be arranged through the Chamber of Mines. Gumboot dancing can also be seen at some of these working mines.

Diamond Cutting Tours

Educational tours available at the Erickson Diamond Centre take you through the cutting process, manufacture, design and setting of the gems. A museum on site also provides information on the history of diamonds in South Africa.

Museums

The city of Johannesburg and its environs has many interesting museums that portray the history and lifestyle of the region.

Museum Africa

Situated between Bree and Wolhuter Streets in Newton, Museum Africa offers an insight into the history of southern Africa from the Stone Age to the present day. Displays include geological specimens, prints, paintings, photographs and artefacts.

Other interesting museums include:

▶ Adler Museum of the History of Medicine
▶ James Hall Museum of Transport
▶ National Museum of Military History
▶ South African Transport Museum

Theatres

There are several theatres within the province offering a wide range of performing arts. Details are available in the local newspaper or from the Publicity Association. Popular venues include the Market, Civic and Alhambra theatres.

Market Theatre

The Market Theatre was built in the early 1900s. Originally a thriving produce market, the complex was saved from demolition by a group of actors who converted it into a theatre. The complex is also home to the French Cultural Institute, the Foundation for Creative Arts and the Newton Art Gallery, as well as Gramadoelas Restaurant and the famous jazz venue, Kippies Bar.

Soweto

The township of Soweto, an acronym for South Western Township, has in recent years become one of the province's most popular tourist attractions. Visitors are advised to take an organised tour in order to enjoy greater insight of the history of the township. Several companies offer daily tours, taking visitors through the various areas from the more affluent suburbs to the shantytowns. Tours include visits to a traditional healer, the Soweto Art Gallery and shebeen-cum-restaurants, which offer a realistic view of life and entertainment in Soweto.

Pretoria

Pretoria is situated some 56km from Johannesburg in the warm and fertile valley of the Apies River. The city of Pretoria is the administrative capital of the country. It is known for its beautiful historic buildings and fine museums that house the country's cultural and artistic treasures. Pretoria is often referred to as 'Jacaranda City' because of the beautiful springtime spectacle of flowering jacaranda trees lining its streets.

Church Square

Church Square is the heart from which the city of Pretoria grew. The original buildings of the Raadsaal (Council Chamber) and Palace of Justice were erected in the late 19th century during the time of President Paul Kruger.

Union Buildings

Towards the north of the city lie the Union Buildings. The honey-coloured sandstone edifices were designed by Sir Herbert Baker and are the headquarters of the government.

▷ *The Union Buildings in Pretoria*

Voortrekker Monument

The Voortrekker Monument stands just outside the city of Pretoria. In designing the monument, its architect, Gerard Moerdijk, was inspired by the Great Zimbabwe ruins.

In the lower hall is an inscribed cenotaph that is illuminated by a shaft of sunlight that shines through an aperture in the roof only at noon on 16 December – the Day of the Vow. This is a date held sacred in the calendar of the Afrikaner people to commemorate victory at the Battle of Blood River in 1838, but in a spirit of patriotism it has been officially renamed as a public holiday observed by all South Africans as the Day of Reconciliation.

The Hall of Heroes has a marble frieze running along its walls for some 92m depicting the main events of the Great Trek. At the entrance to the monument is a bronze statue by the famous South African sculptor, Anton van Wouw, depicting a Voortrekker mother and child. At the four corners are busts of the leaders of the Great Trek – Piet Retief, Andries Pretorius and Hendrik Potgieter – and one of a symbolic nameless leader. Encircling the monument is a wall sculpted with 64 covered Voortrekker wagons symbolic of the *laager* (camp) at the battle. Above the main entrance is the head of a buffalo, regarded as the most dangerous and determined of all animals when wounded.

The nearby Voortrekker Monument Museum contains a selection of Voortrekker memorabilia as well as a set of magnificent tapestries portraying the life of the Voortrekkers.

Tourism Destinations Southern Africa

National Zoological Gardens

The National Zoological Gardens is the largest in South Africa and is regarded as one of the top zoos in the world. Established in 1899, the grounds cover an area of 75ha. The main functions of the zoo are conservation, education, research and the recreational needs of its visitors. It has over 200 mammals and 80 bird species, of which 70 are classified as highly endangered. Apart from its enclosures, which are designed to resemble the animal's natural habitat, there is a walk-through aviary, an animal nursery, veterinary hospital and farmyard area. The zoo has an education programme, which includes courses for adults and for school children during school holidays. Facilities include cable-car rides commanding a superb view over the zoo, a train which transports people to the different sections of the zoo, a restaurant, a conference facility, a souvenir shop, picnic and braai facilities.

Premier Diamond Mine

The town of Cullinan lies some 30km to the east of Pretoria and is home to the Premier Diamond Mine. In 1905 the mine yielded the world's biggest diamond, the 3 106 carat Cullinan Diamond. Tours of the mine are conducted from Tuesdays to Fridays.

Museums

The city of Pretoria and its environs has numerous museums worth visiting.

Places that give one an insight into the lifestyle of another era and a glimpse of the lives of the famous people who lived at that time are:

▶ Melrose House

▶ Kruger House

▶ Sammy Marks Museum

▶ Smuts House Museum

Museums in which are displayed a splendid collection of work by South Africa's leading artists include:

▶ Pierneef Museum

▶ Pretoria Art Museum

▶ Anton van Wouw House

Other interesting museums include:

▶ The Museum of Science and Technology
▶ Transvaal Museum of Natural History

The State Theatre

The State Theatre complex is known for its top-class performances of opera, ballet, theatre and symphony concerts.

Magaliesberg

The Magaliesberg region straddles Gauteng and North West Province. It is known as Cashan Territory and is home to one of the world's most mystifying mountain ranges. Archaeologists have as yet been unable to date the rock engravings in the Magaliesberg mountains and although some suggest they belong to the Late Stone Age, it remains a mystery as to who executed them. In addition, the remains of many small Iron Age villages have been located in the vicinity. The spectacular scenery of the region and wealth of flora and fauna, which includes the Cape vulture and black eagle, make it a favourite spot for nature lovers. It has several popular hiking trails, as well as horse riding and angling opportunities. The village of Magaliesberg nestles in the foothills of the Magaliesberg mountain range and has several curio shops, tea gardens and places of interest.

The area is a favourite weekend retreat for the people of Gauteng/Johannesburg and has several upmarket hotels and country lodges, as well as bed and breakfast, self-catering, caravan and camping facilities. The region has also become well known as a corporate conference venue offering first class accommodation and facilities within a short distance of the city centre.

Historic Sites

Sterkfontein Caves

Situated to the west of Johannesburg, the Sterkfontein Caves are regarded as one of the world's most important anthropological sites. It was in these caves that the palaeontologist, Dr Robert Broom of the Transvaal Museum, discovered the fossilised female skeleton known as 'Mrs Ples' (*Plesianthropus transvaalensis*), estimated to be two and a half million years old. Tours are available that take visitors through the Hall of Elephants, the largest cavern of some 23m high and 91m long, as well as smaller caverns such as the Fairy Chamber and the Graveyard. There is an immense lake situated under the cave system and several dripstone formations can also be seen. Facilities at the caves include a restaurant and small museum.

Wonder Cave

The Wonder Cave at Kromdraai is some 2 200 million years old. Tours are conducted along well-lit pathways, where competent guides point out its strangely shaped formations. Facilities at the cave include an educational centre/ museum and a refreshment kiosk.

Cultural Villages

Lesidi Cultural Village

The Lesidi Cultural Village is situated at the foot of the Magaliesberg mountain range to the north of Johannesburg. The complex houses traditional villages of the Zulu, Xhosa, Pedi and Basotho people and offers visitors a chance to view their culture and way of life whilst walking through the homesteads. Lunchtime and evening visits include tours of the homesteads, traditional singing and dancing and an African feast. Overnight accommodation is available at the village, as well as conference facilities.

Sibaya

Situated a short distance from Sandton, the Sibaya offers visitors an insight into the traditional lifestyle and culture of the Zulu people. Guests are entertained with song, dance and stories, and are offered traditional food and beer.

Phumangena Zulu Village

The Phumangena Zulu Village is located in the Aloe Ridge Hotel and Game Reserve complex. This authentic Zulu village offers an opportunity to experience dancing and singing whilst enjoying traditional food and beer. Other highlights include watching the traditional craftsmen at work, or meeting the resident Sangoma who will throw the bones for you, to foretell the future. Overnight accommodation is available.

Pioneer Open Air Museum

Situated on the outskirts of Pretoria, the museum consists of a thatched Voortrekker farmhouse and a reconstructed pioneer farmyard. Demonstrations of the domestic skills of a typical pioneer household include bread baking, butter churning, soap making and thong dressing (narrow strips of hide used to make halters, reins or lashes for whips). Guided tours are available.

Activity

Draw up a list of the various day trips that can be taken from Johannesburg.

5 MPUMALANGA

Facts at a Glance

Capital	Nelspruit
Size	79 490 sq km
Population	2,8m
Average Temperature	Summer min 19°C/max 30°C
– Nelspruit	Winter min 6°C/max 24°C
Main Languages	English, Afrikaans, siSwati, isiNdebele, xiTsonga, seSotho

Geographical Outline

Located in the north-eastern part of the country, Mpumalanga is bordered by Northern Province to the north, Gauteng to the west, Free State to the south-west, KwaZulu-Natal to the south-east, and Mozambique and the Kingdom of Swaziland to the east.

The region's terrain alters dramatically as one travels eastwards from the flat, grassy Highveld. Passing through the strikingly beautiful mountain ridge that forms part of South Africa's Great Escarpment known as the Transvaal Drakensberg, the Lowveld savannah lies below.

Important rivers include the Crocodile, Olifants, Eland, Sabie and Komati and the main dams within the region are Grootdraai, Jericho and Loskop.

Introduction

The Region

Mpumalanga is one of South Africa's major tourism destinations. It boasts some of the country's most spectacular scenery and has much to offer visitors. A vast tract of the Kruger National Park lies within the borders of the province, as do several adjoining private game reserves. Its history is full of romantic tales of a time when early travellers visited the area in search of ivory, gold and fortune. The region is also a favourite destination for sport and leisure enthusiasts and has recently become a popular venue for adventure tourism.

The Economy

Mpumalanga's principal economic activities are mining, agriculture, forestry, manufacturing and tourism. The economy of the region will be greatly enhanced when the Maputo–Nelspruit corridor is completed. This development includes the expansion and upgrading of the road from Gauteng to Maputo, giving better access to the harbour in Maputo for both imports and exports to the province and the rest of South Africa.

The Importance of Tourism

The regional government considers tourism to be of great importance as a source of employment and revenue and plans are under way for an improved infrastructure and expansion of amenities.

Climate

The climate of the province is as diverse as its scenery although the whole area falls into the summer rainfall region and is prone to late afternoon thunder- and hailstorms. Summer temperatures on the Highveld tend to be hot, but in winter can fall to freezing point, with occasional snow. Mist may occur throughout the year and can be a driving hazard. The subtropical Lowveld plains are often extremely hot in summer and warm and clear in winter.

Transportation and Accessibility

Road

There is an excellent network of tarred roads throughout Mpumalanga. The N4 traverses the region to connect Johannesburg (in Gauteng) with Komatipoort and the southern part of the Kruger National Park via Nelspruit. The N17 passes through Ermelo and Chrissiesmeer and on to the Swaziland border. The N2 connects Ermelo with Piet Retief and KwaZulu-Natal. The N11 passes through the Mpumalanga towns of Middleburg, Ermelo and Volksrust before continuing southwards into KwaZulu-Natal.

Despite the fine road network, it is difficult to reach some of the region's main tourist attractions by local transportation and it is advisable to use own transport or take an organised tour. Car hire services are available at Skukuza Airport and Nelspruit. There is a daily coach service from Johannesburg/Pretoria to Nelspruit and on to Maputo in Mozambique.

Air

Flights operate from Johannesburg International Airport to Nelspruit and Skukuza, and from Nelspruit to Durban and Maputo.

Rail

Mainline trains operate daily from Johannesburg to Komatipoort via Nelspruit. The luxury Rovos Rail operates between Pretoria and Komatipoort with road transport from Komatipoort to Skukuza.

Accommodation

Mpumalanga has a large variety of hotels, country lodges, guesthouses, self-catering and bed and breakfast establishments which offer accommodation varying from four-star to budget. Many of the hotels and lodges offer excellent conference facilities.

Several holiday resorts, timeshare and camping and caravan facilities can also be found throughout the region.

The Kruger National Park offers its visitors several different types of self-contained units as well as camping and caravan facilities.

Luxury accommodation is available at most of the adjoining private game reserves as well as at the Karos Lodge situated just outside Paul Kruger Gate.

Historic Highlights

Archaeological evidence suggests human habitation in the region dating back to 100 000BC.

The region's numerous examples of San rock art are testimony to the San having once lived in the province.

Around AD1400 people from the north moved into Mpumalanga bringing livestock with them and advanced techniques of iron smelting. They built stonewalled settlements.

Between 1836 and 1845, the Boer trekkers arrived in the area.

In 1871 gold was discovered on the farm Geelhoutboom and at Graskop. Other finds at Sabie, Barberton and Pilgrim's Rest heralded gold rush fever and brought people from the world over to the region.

Work on the Eastern Railway Line from Delagoa Bay to Pretoria began around 1887. The railway line brought an end to the era of transport riders.

In 1898 the land between the Crocodile and Sabie rivers was declared a game sanctuary and in 1926 the Kruger National Park was proclaimed.

The province was renamed Mpumalanga in 1994.

Population

The main population groups who inhabit Mpumalanga are the Ndebele, Shangaan, Swazi, North Sotho and people of European descent.

Social and Cultural Profile

The first settlers of European descent were the Voortrekkers, searching for a trading route away from British control. They were followed by other European explorers. Increased trade saw trails forged through the bush and the emergence of transport riders who drove wagonloads of goods to the region's isolated outposts. The discovery of gold brought prospectors to the region, followed by the men who built the railways and the farmers who turned the region into one of the country's richest agricultural centres.

The province has much to offer tourists interested in history, art and culture. Fine museums are located at Lydenburg, Barberton, Pilgrim's Rest and Skukuza. Remnants of the many famous battles that took place throughout the region are found at Middleburg, Lydenburg, Machadodorp and the Long Tom Pass. The province also has several examples of San rock art, as well as the recently discovered archaeological site on the hills above Lydenburg, known as the Lydenburg Heads.

The numerous cultural villages situated within the region give an insight into the lifestyles of the people who have made Mpumalanga their home.

Art

One of the provinces most well-known forms of art is the mural art and beadwork designs of the Ndebele people. Artists such as Emmly and Martha Masanabo are well known for their artistic prowess.

Literature

Stories of life in Mpumalanga during the 1880s have been immortalised in tales such as *Jock of the Bushveld* by Sir Percy Fitzpatrick, which tells the story of the life of a transport rider and his Staffordshire terrier in the Eastern Transvaal before the days of the railway.

Sport and Leisure Facilities

A number of special interest tours are offered throughout Mpumalanga taking in such activities as game viewing, bird watching, river rafting and mountain biking. Individually tailored tours to suit visitors' specific needs can also be arranged. Details are available at tourist information offices throughout the province.

Hiking

Numerous hiking trails and day walks exist throughout the province, varying from easy to difficult. Information on the duration and level of difficulty is available from the tourist information centres. Winter is considered to be the best time to hike in the Lowveld as temperatures are generally too high during the summer months. Popular trails include the five-day Prospector's Trail from Bourke's Luck Potholes to the Mac Mac Forest Station; the five-day Blyderivierspoort Hiking Trail from God's Window to Swadini in the north-eastern part of the Blyde River Nature Reserve; the two- to five-day Fanie Botha Hiking Trail from the Ceylon Forest Station near Sabie; the three-day Gold Nugget Hiking Trail, the two-day Pioneer Trail and the two-day Umvoti Trail which all commence around Barberton. Favourite day walks include the 12km Jock of the Bushveld Trail which commences at Graskop and takes in several views of eroded sandstone mentioned in the story of Jock of the Bushveld; and the Rose Creek Walk and Fortuna Mine Walk which start from the centre of Barberton.

Game Hunting

Hunting is available at several private game farms within the region. The main areas are situated in Piet Retief, Groblersdal, Marble Hall and various parts of the Lowveld.

Fishing

Numerous angling sites situated within the province provide excellent facilities and details of sites are available at tourist information offices. The Highveld Escarpment is a well-established area for trout fishing at centres such as Dullstroom, Machadodorp, Waterval-Boven, Badplaas, Belfast, Lydenburg, Wakkerstroom, Pilgrim's Rest and Sabie. Tiger fishing is popular in the large rivers around Komatipoort. Fishing rods and tackle are available for hire in most areas.

Horse Riding

Horse riding trails are available at Pilgrim's Rest, Sabie, White River and the Kaapschehoop Horse Trails, situated just outside Nelspruit.

Ornithology

The province is an important destination for ornithologists and bird-watchers and tourist information offices located throughout the province provide details on specific sites. The most frequented birding areas are those of the Kruger Park and adjacent game parks, Mthethomusha Nature Reserve, the Loskop Dam Nature Reserve, Wakkerstroom, Gustav Klingbiel Dam, Ohrigstad Dam Reserve, Badplaas, Chrissiesmeer and the Jerico Dam.

River Rafting

River rafting sites can be found near Badplaas, Hazyview, Nelspruit and Blyde River.

Mountain Biking

Mountain biking trails have been laid out through the plantations and indigenous forests around Graskop with a choice of tough and leisurely routes. Trail maps and permits are available from the local tourist office. Other popular venues are to be found near Badplaas, Barberton, Chrissiesmeer, Sabie and Wakkerstroom. Bike hire is provided by several of the region's hotels and guesthouses.

Steam Train Safaris

Rovos Rail offers luxury steam train safaris through the Lowveld and Escarpment from Pretoria to Komatipoort, and the Blue Train operates between Pretoria and Hoedspruit.

Conservation and Eco-Tourism

The province has several organisations involved with conservation and eco-tourism. These are managed at reserves such as the Blyde River Canyon, Loskop Dam and Mthethomusha Nature Reserve, as well as venues such as the Nelshoogte Nature Reserve close to Badplaas, involved with the middleveld environment; the Oribi Reserve near Piet Retief, concerned with the Oribi antelope and certain grassland species; and the Majuba Power Station Nature Reserve near Volksrust, involved in a project on the giant girdled lizard.

Wildlife Parks and Nature Reserves

Kruger National Park

The Kruger National Park is one of the world's most important conservation areas. It was established in 1898 by President Paul Kruger, who realised the importance of conserving the nation's wildlife heritage to enable future generations to enjoy the truly magical experience of seeing African wildlife in its natural habitat.

Part of the money received from visitors to the Kruger National Park is used to help fund the preservation of the park's natural environment. It is also used for research into the behaviour and management of the various animal species.

▷ *A lion of the Kruger National Park*

▷ *A Cheetah kill*

The Kruger Park stretches 350km from north to south and measures 60km at its widest point. The total surface area is 1 948 528ha (21 497 sq km), an area larger than some small countries. Its flora and fauna is immense and diverse and covers several different ecosystems. There are 147 species of mammals, 507 species of bird, 49 species of fish, 33 types of amphibian, 114 reptilian species and some 300 different types of trees. Wildlife roams freely between the Kruger Park and the adjoining private game parks and vegetation is left as far as possible undisturbed by the Kruger Park management.

The region has a subtropical climate with summer rains falling between October and March. Many of the animals give birth to their young at this time of year. Annual rainfall varies from 400mm in the north to 700mm in the south. The lack of water during the winter months brings the animals to the waterholes and rivers and this together with the dry winter vegetation makes game spotting easier.

One of the unique features of the Kruger National Park is that it allows visitors to drive their own vehicles and so discover nature for themselves. This can benefit people with young children as most of the private game parks do not admit children under the age of 12 years and many children do not have the attention span to cope with the long game drives of organised safaris. However, for visitors who are not accustomed to spotting game, or have only a short period of time to visit the parks, organised safaris are often a better option and various tour operators offer guided tours into the park. Guided day and night game drives are available on request from the National Parks Board at most camps.

Accommodation and Facilities

The park offers a variety of accommodation choices including guesthouses, cottages, bungalows, huts and safari tents, as well as camping and caravan facilities. Most of the accommodation units have their own bathrooms and cooking facilities. Caravan and camping sites, with the exception of Balulue, have power points as well as communal kitchen and ablution facilities. Cooking utensils, crockery and cutlery are not provided.

Skukuza is the park's largest rest camp and is the operational and administrative headquarters of the park. Its facilities include an environmental education centre, museum, library, film shows on conservation and wildlife, as well as a doctor, a bank with an ATM, a post office, police station, petrol station, Automobile Association (AA) services, a restaurant, shop, nursery, launderette and a braai (barbecue) area.

Types of Camp

There are three different types of camp throughout the park: the rest camps, bushveld camps and private bush lodge camps.

Rest Camps

The park's main rest camps provide a wide range of accommodation possibilities as well as camping and caravan facilities. All the major camps have electricity, communal kitchen facilities, communal ablution blocks, a shop, a first-aid centre, a laundromat, public telephones, a petrol station, a restaurant and/or self-service cafeteria and braai sites.

Bushveld Camps

The bushveld camps offer more luxurious accommodation in smaller, remote camps and there are no shops or restaurants. Accommodation may be reserved for one or more units and visitors can only enter camps if they have reserved accommodation. All units have private bathroom and cooking facilities. Day and night drives are organised at most of the camps.

Private Bush Lodge Camps

A bush lodge is a private lodge that accommodates between 12–19 persons and must be reserved in its entirety. It allows visitors complete privacy as only residents are allowed into the camps. There are no shops or restaurants but cooking facilities are provided.

Conference Venues

Facilities exist at Berg-en-dal, Jakkalsbessie, Bateleur and Monpani.

Picnic Sites

Picnic sites are dotted throughout the park and most provide toilets, a shop, and braai facilities.

Wilderness Trails

There are several wilderness trails within the Kruger National Park, which give the opportunity to experience nature at close range under the guidance of experienced trail rangers.

Private Game Reserves

The three main private reserves bordering the park are Sabi Sand, Timbavati and Klasarie. Other smaller reserves situated within the region include Thornybush and Manyeleti. The game lodges normally offer early morning and evening game drives and are situated near to water so that visitors can sit on the verandah and watch the wildlife come to drink. Guests can either use their own transportation or be collected from Skukuza, Hoedspruit or Phalaborwa airports, or charter a light aircraft to the lodge's private airstrip. Many of the camps do not take children under the age of 12 years.

The best-known private game lodges are Mala Mala, Sabi Sabi and Londolozi.

The Mala Mala Game Reserve straddles some 50km of the Sand River and is one of the most expensive private lodges in the region. It has an excellent reputation for combining luxury service and game viewing. The reserve comprises three luxury lodges and offers excellent fine cuisine. Game viewing options include game drives and walking safaris accompanied by experienced Shangaan trackers.

The Sabi Sabi Private Game Reserve lies on the banks of the Sabie River within the Sabi Sand Game Reserve. Accommodation consists of three lodges and a tented camp. Game viewing options include drives in open-air vehicles or walking safaris accompanied by qualified rangers and trackers. Delicious meals are served on the dining verandah or in the open-air reed enclosed 'boma'.

Londolozi Game Reserve, set in the Sabi Sand Reserve, is well known for its conservation work. It is considered to be one of the region's finest game lodges, offering luxury accommodation and fine cuisine. Game viewing options include morning or evening game drives in open Land Rovers or bush walks accompanied by experienced rangers.

Gustav Klingbiel Nature Reserve

Situated just before the town of Lydenburg on the top of Mount Anderson, is the 2 200ha Gustav Klingbiel Nature Reserve. The reserve is home to the Lydenburg Museum. The museum follows the history of human development in the region from the Early Stone Age to the present day, and exhibits tools and artefacts from each period, with pride of place given to relics of the Iron Age.

Mount Sheba Nature Reserve

The Mount Sheba Nature Reserve covers an area of some 1 500ha and boasts some magnificent examples of indigenous Drakensberg forest including 110 species of forest tree, as well as several ferns, orchids and cycads. The Mount Sheba Hotel is situated within the reserve and numerous paths lead from the hotel into the forests. Adjoining the reserve is the Mount Sheba Game Sanctuary, which offers self-catering accommodation in an old farmhouse.

Tourist Attractions

Mpumalanga Highveld

The Mpumalanga Highveld covers the region from its border with Gauteng to the edge of the escarpment. The area has several important birding sites and tourist attractions such as the Loskop Dam and Nature Reserve and the Botshabelo Mission Station.

Escarpment

The Escarpment is a region of awe-inspiring scenery and exceptional beauty that encompasses the Transvaal Drakensberg Escarpment for some 300km from the border of Northern Province to Swaziland. The Drakensberg's dramatic eastern face plunges hundreds of metres to the coastal plain of the Lowveld. The towns of Dullstroom, Lydenburg, Machadodorp and Waterval-Boven are situated on its higher reaches whilst Pilgrim's Rest, Sabie and Graskop are nestled on its eastern slopes.

Panorama Route

The Panorama Route is a 70km circular drive that takes in many of the region's most spectacular sights including the Blyde River Canyon, Abel Erasmus Pass, the Pinnacle, God's Window, the Lisbon Falls, the Berlin Falls, Bourke's Luck Potholes and the Three Rondavels.

The Blyde River Canyon

The Blyde River Canyon is a large, sandstone gorge with a sheer cliff face that drops to the Blyde River below. The scenically beautiful canyon is situated within the Blyde River Nature Reserve.

▷ *The Blyde River Canyon*

Pilgrim's Rest

In 1873 the prospector Alec (Wheelbarrow) Patterson discovered gold in the area of Pilgrim's Rest. The town, which still retains much of its history and charm, was declared a national monument in 1974. It has much to offer tourists as several of the old miners' houses have been restored and turned into museums and shops.

▷ *A shop at Pilgrim's Rest*

Mac Mac Falls and Mac Mac Pools

The Mac Mac Falls is a 65m high waterfall considered one of the most scenic in the region. The Mac Mac Pools, a set of natural rock pools situated in a forest setting, are a short distance away from the falls. The pools are a popular swimming and picnic area and their location is the starting point of the four-kilometre Forest Falls Nature Walk.

Long Tom Pass

The Long Tom Pass is historically famous for the battle fought there during the Anglo–Boer War. A replica of a Long Tom cannon used in the battle is positioned at the top of the pass.

Bourke's Luck Potholes

Bourke's Luck Potholes is one of the region's popular tourist stopovers. The unusually shaped circular potholes have been eroded over time by the force of the river. The ravine itself measures 30m at its deepest although most holes are no deeper than 6m. There are paths and footbridges along which visitors can look down into the ravine.

Lydenburg

The Voortrekkers founded Lydenburg (town of suffering) in 1849 after they had journeyed from the malaria-stricken town of Andries-Ohrigstad about 50km to the north-east. They named their new home to commemorate the hardships they had endured. Lydenburg has several of its original old buildings including Voortrekker School (built in 1851), the Voortrekker Church and the Dutch Reformed Church. Other places of interest in the region include the archaeological discovery site of the Lydenburg Heads, and Lydenburg Museum situated in the nearby Gustav Klingbiel Nature Reserve.

Lydenburg Heads

The Lydenburg Heads, a collection of seven clay heads thought to date back to AD490, are a recent find believed to be some of the earliest sculptures of the human form. Replicas of the heads are on display at the Lydenburg Museum and the originals are exhibited at the South African Museum in Cape Town.

Dullstroom

Dullstroom is situated some 2 076m above sea level and is a popular venue for trout fishing. Close to the town lies the Verlorenvallei Nature Reserve, which is home to blue, wattled and crowned crane. The park is also well known for its numerous species of orchid.

Lowveld

The Lowveld covers the region from the Escarpment to the Mozambique border. Most of the country's wildlife parks and reserves are to be found in this lush, sub-tropical region of Mpumalanga.

Sudwala Caves

The caves lie in the Crocodile River Valley and are a major tourist attraction. Visitors can explore the caves' strange formations, which have been given names such as Screaming Monster, the Rocket Silo and the Weeping Madonna. A vast expanse of caverns and tunnels still lie undiscovered beneath the hill known as *Mankalakele* (crag upon crag). Guided tours are available.

Nelspruit

Nelspruit is the provincial capital of Mpumalanga, lying 375 kilometres east of Johannesburg on the N4 highway. The town developed when the railway line was built between Pretoria and Lourenço Marques (now Maputo). It is one of the nation's fastest growing cities and a major agricultural region. Its main tourist attraction is the Lowveld Botanical Gardens, which features over 700 indigenous species and some 1 500 exotic species.

Wetland Region

The relatively unknown southern region of Mpumalanga is an area of exceptional beauty with an abundance of bird life. It is gaining in popularity with hikers, anglers, hang-gliders and mountain bikers. There are several country hotels, guesthouses and bed and breakfast establishments throughout the area, to suit every budget.

Tourism Destinations Southern Africa

Wakkerstroom

Established in 1859, the village of Wakkerstroom lies 2 170m above sea level and is situated in a wetland conservation area for several species of rare birds. It is also a popular venue for trout fishing in the Heyshope and Zaaihoek dams. This favoured wetland tourism area is soon to become a World Heritage Site.

Cultural Villages

There are several cultural villages dotted throughout the province, which portray the lifestyles of the local people. Well-known villages include the Tsonga Kraal in the Hans Merensky Reserve, the Ndebele villages at Loopspruit near KwaMhlanga and Botshabelo near Middleburg, and the Swazi Cultural Village at Matsulu, close to Nelspruit.

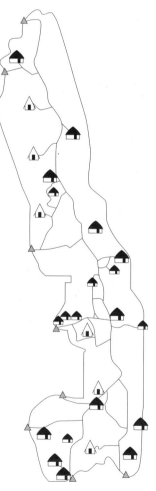

Activity

a. On the given blank map, place the names of the main rest camps and gates of the Kruger National Park.

Main Rest Camps:
Punda Maria, Shingwedzi, Mopani, Letaba, Olifants, Satara, Skukuza, Lower Sabie, Pretoriuskop, Berg-en-dal, Malelane, Crocodile Bridge.

Gates:
Pafuri, Punda Maria, Phalaborwa, Orpen, Paul Kruger, Numbi, Malelane, Crocodile Bridge.

b. What are the fundamental differences between the Kruger National Park and the adjacent private game reserves?

NORTHERN CAPE

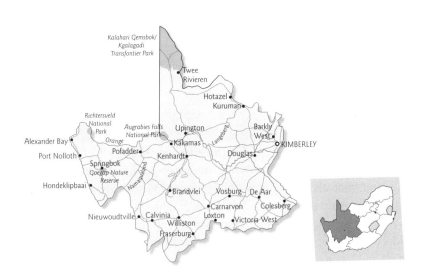

Facts at a Glance

Capital	Kimberley
Size	361 830 sq km
Population	0,84m
Average Temperature – Kimberley	Summer min 18°C/max 32°C Winter min 10°C/max 18°C
Main Languages	Afrikaans, seTswana, isiXhosa, English

Geographical Outline

Located in the north-western corner of the country, Northern Cape shares its border with Namibia, Botswana and North West Province in the north, Free State to the east, Eastern Cape to the south-east and Western Cape to the south. Its western coastline borders the Atlantic Ocean. The Orange River is the most important river in the province and the main mountain ranges include the Roggeveldberge, Nuweveldberge and Asbesberge.

Introduction

The Region

Northern Cape is the largest of South Africa's provinces. It is a region of endless open spaces as well as breathtaking mountain scenery, and is rich in precious stones and minerals. The mighty Orange River flows across much of the province, irrigating the surrounding area and transforming an otherwise barren landscape into fields of lush agricultural produce dotted with prosperous towns and villages.

Much of the appeal of Northern Cape Province lies in its stark, spectacular scenery and fascinating history of diamonds, fame and fortune. It offers the world-weary traveller a delightful alternative holiday destination.

The Economy

The economy of the province is based largely on mining and agriculture. Some of South Africa's richest alluvial diamond deposits are found in the area around Alexander Bay, copper mines exist in the Okiep and Nababeep region and iron and manganese is mined in the Kalahari.

The rich and fertile land around the Orange River Valley produces potatoes, lucerne, wheat, dates, nuts, grains and grapes. It is home to the world's second largest wine cellar, the Orange River Co-operative, and the South African Dried Fruit Co-operative's raisin processing plant.

Other economic sectors include the West Coast crayfish industry at Port Nolloth and sheep farming in the south.

The Importance of Tourism

The region has long been a favourite destination of hikers and nature lovers, especially Namaqualand, famous for its indigenous flora – in springtime the countryside is carpeted with magnificent displays of wild flowers, which is a great tourist attraction. The area has also become a popular adventure tourism venue and there are several 4 x 4 trails and mountain biking tracks to be found throughout the region.

Climate

The Northern Cape's weather is typical of desert and semi-desert regions, with little rainfall and high summer temperatures. Winter days are warm but temperatures drop dramatically during the night. Fog often occurs along the coastline. The best time to visit the region is during the spring and autumn months.

Transportation and Accessibility

Road

There are several main highways traversing the province and connecting all the major centres. The N7 runs parallel to the coast from Cape Town to the Namibian border, connecting at Springbok with the N14, which runs eastwards to Pretoria via Upington and Kuruman. The N10 (from Port Elizabeth) crosses into the province from Middelburg (Eastern Cape) through De Aar, Prieska, Groblershoop and Upington and on to the Namibian border. Linking with the N10 at Groblershoop, the R64 passes eastward through Grigquatown and Campbell to Kimberley, and on via Boshof to Bloemfontein in Free State. The N12 from Johannesburg in the north, passes southward through Kimberley, Hopetown, Britstown, and Victoria West before its joins up with the main N1 highway en route to Cape Town.

There are several bus and coach companies serving the region and car hire operations are located in Kimberley, Upington and Springbok.

Air

Air services operate between Johannesburg and Upington/Kimberley, Cape Town and Springbok/Upington/Kleinzee and Alexander Bay.

Rail

There is a rail network throughout the province and several mainline trains serve the region. The luxury Blue Train and Rovos Rail services traverse part of the province on their journeys between Johannesburg and Cape Town. Rovos Rail offers a visit to the Big Hole during its stopover at Kimberley.

Accommodation

Accommodation in the region consists mainly of small hotels, guesthouses, bed and breakfast and self-catering establishments, as well as caravan and camp sites. Most of the game parks and nature reserves provide accommodation. Traditional dome-shaped reed huts afford visitors an opportunity to experience aspects of the Nama culture, at Namastad in Namaqualand.

Historic Highlights

In 1685 Simon van der Stel led an expedition into the area that is now known as Northern Cape Province after reports from the Nama people that large copper deposits were to be found to the north of the Cape Colony. Deposits were found at Springbok, but were too deep to mine at that time and mining in the area only began in 1852.

In the early part of the 19th century, missionaries travelled to the interior of the land establishing a number of mission stations. They built homes, churches and schools and brought Christianity to the people.

In 1866, 15-year-old Erasmus Jacobs found a 'stone' on the banks of the Orange River, close to present-day Hopetown, which later became known as the 'Eureka' diamond. Some three years later the diamond known as the 'Star of South Africa' was found by a Griqua shepherd, and in 1871 the diamond-rich kimberlite 'pipes' were discovered on a hill known as the Colesburg Kopje, which is today commonly referred to as the Big Hole.

The discovery of diamonds and the wealth it brought to the region played a major role in the growth of Kimberley and the nation's economy.

During the Anglo–Boer War the Northern Cape region was the scene of many famous battles, such as the Siege of Kimberley.

Population

The population of Northern Cape consists mainly of Tswana, Griqua, San and people of Asian and European origin.

Social and Cultural Profile

The people of Northern Cape Province are an eclectic mix. Some are the descendants of the early European settlers, others came to the area to mine and together with the indigenous people of the region have made the province their home. Most are Afrikaans speaking and work mainly in the mining or agricultural sectors of the economy.

Sport and Leisure Facilities

Countless sport and leisure possibilities exist within the province, including hiking, 4 x 4 trails, canoeing, mountain biking, fishing and horse riding.

Hiking

There are numerous hiking trails throughout the province and detailed information is available at information centres. Popular trails include the Pofadder Trail at Pella, the Ian Meyers Hiking Trail in the Goegap Nature Reserve, the Rooiberg Hiking Trail east of Garies and the Klipspringer Trail which follows the Orange River through the Augrabies Falls gorge.

4 x 4 Trails

Popular 4x4 trails include the Namakwa Route, which starts at the mission station of Pella and follows the Orange River over a distance of some 642km, to the diamond mining town of Alexander Bay, and trails through the Richtersveld Desert.

Cycling Trails

Mountain biking has become one of the region's most popular sports. In Namaqualand, mountain biking routes have opened up areas that had been largely undiscovered due to their lack of accessibility. Popular routes in this region include the Nourivier Dam, the Leliefontein Mission Station, Visserplaat and the Goegap Nature Reserve.

Canoe Trails

Several canoe trails operate along the Orange River allowing participants a chance to view the splendour of the landscape via the waterways.

White Water Rafting Trail

A white water rafting trail exists on the Orange River in the vicinity of Hopetown.

Camel Safaris

Camel safari tours operate into the semi-arid region of Northern Bushmanland.

Conservation and Eco-Tourism

The conservation and preservation of the region's fragile ecosystems is of great importance in Northern Cape. Several parks and nature reserves, such as Augrabies Falls National Park, Richtersveld National Park, Kalahari Gemsbok Park/Kgalagadi Transfrontier Park, Tswalu Private Desert Reserve and the Skilpad Wildflower Reserve, provide a sanctuary for wildlife and protect the region's indigenous flora.

Wildlife Parks and Nature Reserves

Augrabies Falls National Park

The Augrabies Falls National Park was created in 1966 to protect and conserve the waterfall and surrounding area. The park's main attraction is the Augrabies waterfall where the Orange River plunges some 56m into a gorge on its way to the Atlantic Ocean. When the river is in flood, Augrabies is one of the world's most awesome waterfalls. There is a suspension bridge over the falls, providing a panoramic view.

Flora able to survive in this low rainfall region includes the kokerboom, camel-thorn and the Karoo boerbean. Fauna to be found within the park is black rhino, eland, monkeys, baboon and various species of antelope.

The park's rest camp provides accommodation in self-contained chalets, as well as facilities for caravans and camping. Other amenities include a restaurant and a museum.

Kalahari Gemsbok National Park/
Kgalagadi Transfrontier Park (KTP)

The Kalahari Gemsbok National Park is situated in the far northern region of the province, some 900km from Johannesburg. The park was proclaimed in 1931 to protect migratory game, especially the gemsbok, and runs adjacent to the Gemsbok National Park in Botswana. The area has recently become southern Africa's first formal transfrontier conservation area. On 7 April 1999 the presidents of Botswana and South Africa signed a historic treaty linking the two parks. The park has been renamed the Kgalagadi Transfrontier Park (KTP) and covers an area of 37 991 sq km.

▷ *Gemsbok in the Kalahari Gemsbok National Park/Kgalagadi Transfrontier Park*

The park's terrain consists of red dunes, sparse vegetation and dry riverbeds. The animals that inhabit the region include the magnificent Kalahari lion, cheetah, leopard, gemsbok, springbok, eland and blue wildebeest, as well as numerous species of birds of prey.

Situated in an arid region with little rainfall, summer daytime temperatures often exceed 40°C. Winters are sunny but night temperatures often fall below zero.

The park is fairly remote and the final stretches are along untarred roads. There are two main roads that follow the dry riverbeds of the Nossob and Auob rivers, with connecting roads across the dunes at two points. There are three rest camps – Twee Rivieren, Mata Mata and Nossob – as well as several rest stops that provide picnic or braai (barbecue) facilities. Twee Rivieren is the largest camp and administrative base and has a restaurant, information centre, car hire collection point and swimming pool.

Accommodation in the camps consists of self-contained cottages and huts as well as camp and caravan sites. Each camp has facilities that include those for laundry, and petrol and diesel supply. Provisions in the shops are often sparse and it is advisable to take all necessary supplies with you, especially camera film and equipment. Visitors to the park are advised to take precautions against malaria. Light aircraft may land at Twee Rivieren, although prior permission must be obtained.

▷ *Accommodation at Twee Rivieren Camp*

Tswalu Private Desert Reserve

The 1 100 sq km Tswalu Private Desert Reserve is situated at the foot of the Korannaberg mountains bordering the Kalahari desert. The reserve is home to some 40 different species of game and runs a combination of extensive breeding programmes and an animal rehabilitation project, including the breeding herd of endangered black rhino, king cheetah, roan and sable antelope.

The reserve offers five-star classic African style accommodation, horse riding and walking trails among the animals, an information centre, swimming pool, curio shop and its own private runway, which is served daily by a charter service from Lanseria airport, close to Johannesburg.

Conference facilities exist for a maximum of 40 delegates. The organisers specialise in 'bush conferences' and incentive groups and offers activities such as treasure hunts, tracking competitions, mountain hiking and orienteering – a competitive sport in which participants cross open country with a map and compass.

Richtersveld National Park

Richtersveld National Park is considered by many to be South Africa's last true wilderness. Its landscape is made up of rugged mountain ranges interspersed with wide sandy plains. Some of the richest succulent plant diversity in the world is found here, with some 50 per cent of the plant species endemic to the Richtersveld and surrounding area. Temperatures can exceed 50°C during the summer and it is advisable to avoid visiting the region during these months. The land receives little rainfall, although the western part is frequently covered in coastal fog, known locally as *malmokkie* (literally, guinea-pig).

The northern section of the Richtersveld was declared a National Park in August 1991. There are two guesthouses at Sendelingsdrif and five designated campsites throughout the rest of the park. Semi-nomadic descendants of the Nama people still live in the region and maintain a fairly traditional lifestyle.

Skilpad Wildflower Reserve

Situated to the west of Kamieskroon, just off the N7 highway, the 1 000ha Skilpad Wild Flower Reserve is considered to be one of the best places to view Namaqualand's spring flowers – it is open to the public only during this period. The reserve was established in 1988 by WWF South Africa (World-Wide Fund for Nature) to conserve the indigenous flora and fauna and increase awareness of Namaqualand's floral heritage. Situated on the first ridge of hills in from the coast, the countryside benefits from the rain that blows in off the sea. It is after the first spring rains that the fields burst into flower.

Goegap Nature Reserve

Situated just 15km south-east of Springbok is the Goegap Nature Reserve. The reserve supports close on 600 indigenous plant species, 45 mammals and 94 different types of bird. Facilities exist for picnicking, hiking, horse trails, 4x4 trails and mountain biking.

Tourist Attractions

Diamond Route

The Diamond Route lies from Victoria West through Hopetown, Kimberley and Warrenton, to Potchefstroom in North West Province.

Kimberley

Kimberley is well known for diamonds and famous men such as Cecil John Rhodes and Barney Barnato. The town has several places of interest, the best known being the Kimberley Mine, popularly called the 'Big Hole'. The Kimberley Mine Museum

incorporates the Big Hole and numerous old buildings, which have been carefully restored to depict the lifestyle and atmosphere of the mining village that grew up around the Big Hole. Exhibits provide information and insight into the workings of the mine and replicas of the most famous diamonds found in the region are displayed in the Diamond Hall.

The Kimberley Tram, styled after the original models in use at the beginning of the century, was reintroduced in 1985 and operates between the Mine Museum and City Hall. Other places worth visiting include the Railway Museum on Kimberley Station, the McGregor Museum, the William Humphreys Art Gallery, the Duggan-Cronin Gallery and the Memorial to the Pioneers of Aviation.

▷ *The Big Hole at Kimberley*

The city has two drive-in pubs – the Halfway House Hotel and the Kimberlite Hotel – believed to be the only two in the world. In a bygone age, such as the era of Rhodes, men rode into the bar on horseback. Today customers order their drinks without leaving their cars.

▷ *The Kimberley Tram*

▷ *Kokerboom, or quiver tree*

Namaqualand

The Namaqualand region is one of Northern Cape's main tourist attractions. After the spring rains, the dry barren landscape is transformed into a kaleidoscope of brilliant colours as the wild flowers bloom. The region is also known for the variety of succulents and unusual trees. Included is the *halfmens* (half man), peculiar to northern Namaqualand and resembling a man when viewed from a distance – the tree is the subject of many legends among the Nama; the *kokerboom* or quiver tree, whose bark was used by the San to make quivers; and the *sterboom* or star-tree, which grows only on the southern sides of the Nuweveld mountains.

There are several suggested flower routes, which ensure visitors take in as much of the splendour of the region as possible. The displays are usually at their peak from early August to the middle/end of September and are best viewed on sunny days between 11:00 and 16:00 – the flowers present their faces to the sun and should be viewed by walking or driving with the sun behind one's back. For optimum viewing details visitors should telephone the Flower Line at (021) 4183705.

Mission Stations

There are still a number of mission stations that operate in Namaqualand, such as Pella, Matjieskloof, Steinkopf and Leliefontein.

Kalahari

Kuruman

The town of Kuruman is a popular stopover point where provisions can be bought at its shops before visiting the more remote and isolated regions of the country. Its main tourist attraction is the 'eye', a small lake formed where a perennial dolomite spring reaches the surface. The spring is so powerful that the rate remains constant even in periods of drought. The source delivers some 10 million litres of water daily and is the biggest natural fountain in the southern hemisphere.

Moffat Mission

The Moffat Mission is situated at Seodin, just outside of Kuruman. The mission was established by the London Missionary Society in 1816 and was moved to its present site in 1825. The original homestead, built by the famous missionary Robert Moffat, is the oldest building north of the Orange River. Many of the mission's historic features have been carefully restored and include the Wagon House – a national monument – which serves as the visitors' reception area and bookshop; the reconstruction of a 1905 classroom that houses the Moffat Press, which printed the first Bible in Africa; the Livingstone Rooms where the famous missionary/explorer stayed in 1853; and the church where the Moffat's daughter Mary married David Livingstone in 1938.

Robert and his wife Mary arrived in the area around 1921 and worked among the Batswana people for many years. It was during this time that Moffat translated and printed the Bible in Tswana.

Roaring Sands

The Roaring Sands are situated in the vicinity of the Padkloof Pass near Postmasburg. The dunes make a noise that varies from a low hum to a loud roar if the surface is disturbed. Fulgurites, a rocky substance caused by flashes of lightning that strike and fuse (vitrify) the sand, are found on the dunes.

Historic Sites

Archaeological Sites

Archaeological excavations carried out at the Wonderwerk Cave close to Danielskuil have revealed significant finds that include a wide range of Later Stone Age artefacts, which are now housed at the McGregor Museum in Kimberley.

San Rock Art Sites

There are numerous sites where San rock art can be viewed, especially in the Bo-Karoo region. Information on sites can be obtained from the local publicity offices or tourism centres.

Activity

Plan an itinerary for a one-day stopover in Kimberley. List six of the city's main attractions.

7 FREE STATE

Facts at a Glance

Capital	Bloemfontein
Size	129 480 sq km
Population	2,6m
Average Temperature	Summer min 15°C/max 31°C
– Bloemfontein	Winter min –2°C/max 16°C
Main Languages	seSotho, Afrikaans, English

Geographical Outline

Free State borders Northern Cape to the west, North West Province, Gauteng and Mpumalanga to the north, KwaZulu-Natal and Lesotho to the east, and Eastern Cape to the south. The region is home to numerous rivers and dams including the Vaal, Orange, Caledon, Wilge and Modder rivers and the Vaal, Bloemhof, Sterkfontein and Gariep dams. Mountain ranges found within the area include the Maluti and Drakensberg.

The region lies some 1 300m above sea level and consists of endless flat plains of rich fertile land. To the east the landscape changes into a spectacularly scenic series of sandstone hills.

Introduction

The Free State landscape gladdens my heart, no matter what my mood. When I am here I feel that nothing can shut me in, that my thoughts can roam as far as the horizons.

Nelson Mandela
Long Walk to Freedom

The Region

Situated between the rivers of the Vaal in the north and the Orange to the south, the landlocked Free State is South Africa's third largest province. The region has been the site of many a historic battle between African, Boer and British and has played a major role in the founding of the Afrikaner Nation.

The Economy

The province is known as South Africa's breadbasket. It has a thriving farming industry of wheat, maize, dairy, cattle and sheep, while the Ficksburg region produces 90 per cent of the country's cherry crop. Mining and quarrying are the largest economic sectors and rich deposits of gold, uranium, coal and bentonite are found in the northern reaches.

The Importance of Tourism

Although Free State is not a main tourist destination, efforts are underway to develop tourism potential. Established tourist venues include the Golden Gate National Park, the historic Anglo–Boer War battlefields, the QwaQwa Conservation Area and the Basotho Cultural Village. The province has a rich historical and cultural heritage and boasts some of the country's most spectacular scenery.

Climate

The region has summer rains, plenty of sunshine and cold dry winters when snow is often found on the mountains of the eastern region.

Transportation and Accessibility

Road

Several of the nation's major road networks pass through the province. The N1 crosses the region linking Northern and Western Cape provinces with Gauteng and Northern Province; the N5 connects with the N1 just outside Winburg, crossing the eastern Free State at Bethlehem and Harrismith where it joins up with the main Johannesburg–Durban route, the N3. The N8 connects Bloemfontein with Lesotho, via Thaba 'Nchu and Ladybrand, and the N6 takes the southerly route from Bloemfontein to East London in Eastern Cape via Smithfield.

Coaches operate from Bloemfontein to all major centres throughout the country, and car hire is available in the main cities of the province.

Air

Bloemfontein Airport has daily return flights to all central airports across the country.

Rail

There is an extensive rail network and several of the mainline trains traverse the province.

Accommodation

Accommodation throughout the province is plentiful. There are several large holiday resorts, numerous hotels, including the Thaba 'Nchu Sun Hotel and Casino and the Naledi Sun Hotel and Casino, guesthouses, guest farms, camp and caravan parks, as well as lodgings in several nature reserves.

Historic Highlights

The Voortrekkers from the Cape, looking for a land free of British domination, arrived in the region after 1835.

Free State (formerly Orange Free State) played a major role in the 1899–1902 Anglo–Boer War.

Population

Although the province has an eclectic mix of peoples who have settled within its borders, the region's main cultural groups are Afrikaners and Basotho.

Social and Cultural Profile

Free State people are known for their hospitality and friendliness. Many of the towns have a fascinating mix of British and Afrikaans culture, evident in its public buildings, monuments and museums, while traditional Basotho houses dot the countryside.

Sport and Leisure Facilities

The province has numerous nature reserves and dams which offer visitors a chance to enjoy the natural environment and partake in various leisure activities such as game viewing, bird watching, fishing and water sports. It is also a popular venue for hiking, mountaineering, mountain biking, 4 x 4 trails and horse riding.

▷ *Horse riding in Free State*

Hiking

Free State boasts a wide variety of hiking opportunities ranging from day walks to 5-day trails and covering a vast range of different terrain and vegetation. Popular trails include the 5-day, 70km Brandwater Hiking Trail and the 2-day, 30km Rhebok Hiking Trail.

Conservation and Eco-Tourism

The natural surroundings and features of the province have facilitated development of the eco-tourism industry in the region. Many of its nature and game reserves offer the opportunity to enjoy the pristine environment.

Wildlife Parks and Nature Reserves

Golden Gate Highlands National Park

The 11 600ha Golden Gate Highlands National Park nestles in the foothills of the Maluti Mountains in the eastern Free State. The park is a most popular tourist attraction and is renowned for its scenic beauty, especially its variety of colourful hues during the autumn period. Summer temperatures are often cooled by thunderstorms and winters tend to be cold with occasional snow.

Activities available at the park include the 2-day Rhebok Hiking Trail, nature trails, game viewing, guided excursions and night drives, environmental educational courses and a variety of sport facilities. Within the park environs are several species of antelope, Burchell's zebra and many birds, including the rare lammergier (bearded vulture) and bald ibis. Accommodation is available in the Brandwag and Glen Reenen rest camps or at the Wilgenhof Hostel, and there are camp and caravan sites at Glen Reenen. Other facilities include a picnic and braai (barbecue) area, curio shop, restaurant and coffee shop, and amenities for conferences and other functions.

▷ *Spectacular scenery of the Golden Gate Highlands National Park*

Maria Moroka National Park

The Maria Moroka National Park covers an area of some 3 400ha and is situated about 10km from the town of Thaba 'Nchu. The park is home to several species of antelope and over 200 species of bird. Facilities available include hiking and mountain bike trails, angling at the Groothoek Dam, horse riding, game drives, and picnic and braai sites.

QwaQwa Highlands National Park

Adjoining the Golden Gate National Park, the QwaQwa park is 22 000ha in extent and its surroundings are characterised by colourful sandstone formations. Several species of antelope and rare birds, such as the black eagle and Cape and bearded vulture, are to be seen. Activities available within the park include game viewing, horse riding and hiking.

Seekoevlei Nature Reserve

The Seekoevlei Nature Reserve, situated to the north of the town of Memel, is considered to have one of the widest varieties of bird species in the country. It is listed under Wetlands of International Importance and endangered birds such as the blue crane, wattled crane and crowned crane can be seen from watchtowers in the reserve.

Tourist Attractions

Central Region

Bloemfontein

Bloemfontein (spring of flowers) is the judicial capital of South Africa and the capital city of Free State Province. The city is affectionately known as the City of Roses and has many places of interest – Naval Hill, the National Museum (housing natural history exhibits), the First Raadsaal (council chamber), the War Museum (the main Anglo–Boer War Museum in South Africa), the Queen's Fort Military Museum, the Anglican Cathedral, and the city's best-known monument, the National Women's Memorial (*Vroue-monument*). The monument was built

▷ *The National Women's Memorial in Bloemfontein*

to commemorate more than 26 000 Boer women and children who died in the Anglo–Boer War, mostly in concentration camps. There are several historic buildings in President Brand Street, such as the City Hall, the Fourth Raadsaal (a late-Victorian architectural gem), the Provincial High Court, and the Appellate Division of the High Court – South Africa's final Court of Appeal.

The Franklin Game Reserve, Botanical Garden, Bloemfontein Zoo, Swart Park and Kings Park offer visitors a chance to enjoy the flora and fauna of the region.

Thaba 'Nchu

Situated some 60km from Bloemfontein is the town of Thaba 'Nchu, named after the 2 138m high Thaba 'Nchu mountain. The mountain was once the stronghold of the Baralong people who inhabited the region in the 1830s. During the Great Trek several parties, including those of Hendrik Potgieter, Piet Uys, Gerrit Maritz and Karel Landman, used the town as a stopover point. In 1979 the town and surrounding area became part of the territory of Bophuthatswana until reincorporated into South Africa in 1994.

The Thaba 'Nchu Sun Hotel and Casino, the Naledi Sun Hotel and Casino, the Maria Moroka National Park and the Rustfontein Nature Reserve are all located within the region. Activities available in the area include game drives, hiking trails, mountain biking and angling at the Groothoek Dam and Rustfontein Dam.

▷ *Thaba 'Nchu Sun Hotel*

Eastern Highlands

Clarens

The picturesque town of Clarens, situated below the sandstone peaks of the Rooiberge, is a favourite stopover. A number of artists have moved into this beautiful setting and have opened up their studios to the public. Other attractions are the several popular hiking and horse riding trails in the area.

Zastron

The town of Zastron lies at the foot of the Aasvoelberg, Free State's highest peak at 2 207m. The area is famous for the 'Eye of Zastron', a hole measuring 9m in diameter in the cliffs of the mountain. The town and surrounding area has several historic monuments, fine examples of sandstone architecture, and San painting that includes examples in the Hippopotamus Cave and a 5m high San frieze on the Glen Rosa Farm. The region also has three dams offering a variety of water sport and fishing opportunities.

Southern Region

Philippolis

The town of Philippolis is the oldest settlement in Free State. It was established as a mission station in 1823 by the London Missionary Society, mainly for the Khoikhoi and San nomads displaced by the closure of the Toverberg (Colesberg) mission in 1818.

In 1825 a school was founded in the town for Griqua nomads. Two years later Dr Phillip of the London Missionary Society presented the area between the Modder and the Orange rivers to the Griqua chief, Adam Kok, on the condition that he protect the mission.

In 1862 the Orange Free State Government bought the region from the Griqua. This gave rise to the historic trek of 1863, when Adam Kok led 2 000 burghers over a distance of 500km to cross the Drakensberg in to Griqualand East (since renamed Kokstad) where they settled.

Historic Sites

Archaeological Sites

The province has many sites dating back to ancient times. In the area around the town of Cornelia, stone tools left by ancient man have been uncovered as well as fossils of pigs, species of extinct antelope, a subspecies of hippo, a giant buffalo and four species of horse. Near to the town of Ladybrand, fossil discoveries have been unearthed at Tripolitania Farm, and in the district surrounding Fauresmith, Stone Age implements and artefacts have been discovered.

San Rock Art Sites

Several examples of San rock art may be viewed throughout the province. Some of the best specimens are to be found on the farms Koesberg, Houtberg and Sterkstroom in the Rouxville district and in the ancient caves in the hills around the Zastron area.

Anglo–Boer War Battlefields

Several towns in the region bear testimony to their involvement in the Anglo–Boer War. Historic sites can be found at towns such as Lindley, Surrender Hill, the Jammerbergdrif battle site close to Wepener, and the Mostertshoek Battlefield near

Reddersburg. The Magersfontein Battlefield and Museum is situated in the area surrounding Jacobsdal. The Paardeberg Anglo–Boer War Musuem and Battlefield lies some 23km outside the town of Petrusburg, and several of the monuments of Springfontein attest to the struggle and hardships of the Anglo–Boer War. The concentration camp, its cemetery and the separate cemetery for the children who died in the camp bear mute testimony to these events of history.

Cultural Villages

Basotho Cultural Village

The Basotho Cultural village is situated in the QwaQwa Highlands National Park. The village depicts the history, lifestyle and architecture of the South Sotho people and allows a glimpse into their way of life. Here you are invited to sample traditional food and beer whilst being entertained with music and dance. A walking trail through the veld habitat of the village is led by a social ecologist and a *ngaka* (healer) who explain the various uses of the grasses, roots and herbs, leaves and bark found along the way. It is also possible to arrange a tour of the most scenic spots of the QwaQwa Highlands National Park on a Basotho pony.

Activity

Your clients would like to spend one week visiting the Eastern Highlands region of Free State. Which attractions would you recommend they visit? Suggest an itinerary that takes in a different venue/activity for each day.

KWAZULU-NATAL

Facts at a Glance

Capital	Pietermaritzburg and Ulundi
Size	92 100 sq km
Population	8,4m
Average Temperature	Summer max 27°C/min 20°C
– Durban	Winter max 22°C/min 11°C
Main Languages	isiZulu, English, Afrikaans, German, Hindi, Tamil, Gujarati, Urdu

Geographical Outline

The province of KwaZulu-Natal shares its northern border with Mpumalanga and the international borders of Mozambique and Swaziland. To the west lie Free State and the Kingdom of Lesotho, and Eastern Cape to the south. The eastern seaboard of KwaZulu-Natal is washed by the warm waters of the Indian Ocean. The Drakensberg Mountains run along its western border with Lesotho. There are numerous important rivers criss-crossing the region, the most important being the Tugela, Mooi, Umkhomaas and Umzimkulu. There are several large lakes, including Lake St Lucia and Lake Sibaya. KwaZulu-Natal is served by the important ports of Durban and Richard's Bay.

Introduction

The Region

KwaZulu-Natal is a province of magnificent scenic beauty, with a wealth of history and a rich cultural heritage infused by Zulu, British, Afrikaner and Indian traditions. The region was named 'Terra de Natalia' by Vasco da Gama who caught sight of the coastline on Christmas Day in 1497.

The Economy

The main economic sectors are mining, manufacturing, and agricultural products such as sugar-cane, pineapples and bananas. Durban harbour is the largest on the African continent and ranks ninth in the world. Tourism plays a major role in the region's economy, attracting a significant percentage of the country's domestic and international tourists.

The Importance of Tourism

The province is one of the country's main tourist destinations. Its diverse attractions range from the Drakensberg mountain region to the many coastal resorts situated to the north and south of Durban. The province has several wildlife parks and nature reserves, covering an immense variety of habitats and ecosystems.

The region is fast becoming a leading light in the promotion of tourism at grass roots and the upliftment of rural communities. Plans are underway for the development of centres in close proximity to existing tourist attractions, allowing visitors to view and appreciate the region's cultural heritage.

Climate

The climate of the province varies dramatically due to the varying altitude. The coastal region has a subtropical climate with warm and pleasant winters and hot and humid summers. The warm coastal waters ensure swimming in the sea throughout the year as the sea temperature rarely falls below 17°C. Inland, the climate is more temperate, although snow is often found on the Drakensberg mountain region during the winter months and weather conditions can change rapidly in the mountains. The entire region falls into a summer rainfall area.

Transportation and Accessibility

Road

There is an extensive network of good roads throughout most of the province. The N3 highway connects Durban with Johannesburg via Pietermaritzburg. The N2 cuts south from the Swaziland border to the Richard's Bay area then follows the coastline through Durban to Port Shepstone where it turns inland to the Eastern Cape border. Many untarred secondary roads towards the northern region of the province are sometimes in poor condition due to heavy rainfalls in the area.

Inter-city coaches link all major centres with Durban and there are fairly good bus and coach services operating throughout the province. Car hire facilities exist in the main centres and airports.

Air

The province's main airport is situated some 16km south of Durban's city centre and operates frequent scheduled flights to most of the country's main centres including Johannesburg and Cape Town. Other airports within the region include Pietermaritzburg, Ulundi and Richard's Bay. Light aircraft, charter flights and helicopters operate out of Virginia airport which is situated some 12km north of the city centre.

Rail

Mainline trains operate between Durban and Johannesburg and Cape Town. There is also a metro service that operates along the South Coast, and the Banana Express steam train, which operates between Port Shepstone and Paddock.

Accommodation

The province provides all categories of accommodation ranging from luxury hotels and lodges to caravan and camp sites. The coastal region offers a wide-ranging choice, with many hotels, resorts, timeshare and self-catering apartments dotted along its entire coastline. Accommodation facilities in the parks and reserves are varied and cater for all tastes, including luxury lodges, fully equipped bungalows, chalets, rustic bush camps and huts. Farm holiday accommodation is also very popular inland, as is bed and breakfast accommodation. The Drakensberg mountain region has an extensive range of accommodation varying from luxury hotels and lodges to simple bed and breakfast and camping facilities. There are also several traditional villages that offer overnight guest accommodation, such as at the Shakaland authentic Zulu village run by Protea Hotels and at Kwabhekithunga – Stewarts Farm. Conference facilities exist in many of the region's large hotels, as well as at the well-equipped International Convention Centre in Durban.

Historic Highlights

The San people were the first people known to have inhabited the region.

The Portuguese navigator Vasco da Gama first sighted the coastline on Christmas Day 1497 and named the area Natal (meaning birth), to mark the day of discovery in association with the birth date of Christ.

The Nguni people are believed to have lived in the Zululand area since the 16th century.

In 1815 Shaka acceded to the Zulu chieftaincy and transformed the nation into one of the most powerful in the region.

The first Europeans to have inhabited the region were survivors of the ships wrecked along the coastline.

In 1824 the British sent a small group of settlers to the region.

In 1838 a group of Voortrekkers under the leadership of Piet Retief arrived in Natal.

In 1842 the British sent troops into the area and shortly thereafter the province was annexed into the Cape Colony.

The region was the scene of many bloody battles between the Zulu, British and Boer.

During the 1860s large numbers of indentured Indian labourers were brought in to work in the sugar-cane plantations.

The province was home to Mahatma Gandhi for several years from 1893. During his stay he founded the Natal Indian Congress and used his philosophy of 'passive resistance' to campaign for social and political reform and against the immigration laws. After the agreement that culminated in the Indian Relief Act in 1914, Gandhi returned to his native land to embark on the struggle for Indian independence.

Population

The population of KwaZulu-Natal is predominantly Zulu, but also includes people of Asian and European descent.

Social and Cultural Profile

Many nations played a significant role in the history and development of KwaZulu-Natal, and their different lifestyles have made the province the culturally rich region it is today. The area known as Zululand has been the home of the Zulu people since the beginning of the 16th century. Their reigning monarch is King Goodwill Zwelatini, who holds the highest military and judicial position. Today, the impact of Zulu culture is felt throughout the province.

▷ *A Zulu warrior and a Zulu woman adorned with traditional bead necklaces*

While English and Afrikaans-speaking people live throughout the region, several pockets of the province have a distinctly Germanic feel about them. Wartburg in the Midlands is home to many fourth-generation Germans who arrived in the region around the mid-19th century and have retained much of their language, culture and lifestyle. Another large German community has lived in the Luneberg region for over six generations and there are several German guesthouses at Paulpietersburg and Vryheid.

The people of Asian descent in the province have maintained much of their culture and traditional ways and celebrate their identity in festivals such as Diwali (or Deepawali), a Hindu festival of lights. Languages spoken are Hindi, Tamil, Urdu and various dialects of Gujarati, however, as the community has become more westernised the predominant language spoken is English.

Sport and Leisure Facilities

The entire KwaZulu-Natal region boasts countless opportunities for enjoying a wealth of outdoor activities. Water sport enthusiasts can indulge their preferences along the extensive stretch of coastline and hikers and bird-watchers will find an inexhaustible choice of venues throughout the inland region.

Cricket is played at the Kingsmead Stadium, rugby at the Kings Park Rugby Stadium, and soccer at the Kings Park Football Stadium. Horseracing takes place at Clairwood Park, Scottsville and Greyville.

Hiking

Popular walking and hiking venues are the Dlinza Forest, close to Eshowe, well known for its hiking trails and picnic spots, and the area around Mpushini Falls. In addition, Paulpietersburg has two walking trails of interest – the Nchaga Trail which passes through the Pongola bush, home to the rare Samango monkey, and the Dumbe Walking Trail, developed by the Publicity Association and used to teach the concept of eco-tourism in rural schools. The Drakensberg mountain region has numerous guided and self-guided trails that vary from strenuous to a pleasant stroll. One of the most popular mountain walks in the northern Berg region is the path to the foot of the Tugela Falls. The walk commences at the Royal Natal National Park and climbs up the Tugela Gorge to a chain ladder that takes you over the final stretch, from where the spectacular view of the falls rushing down the Amphitheatre awaits you.

Wilderness Trails

The KwaZulu-Natal Nature Conservation Service offers wilderness trails in the Hluhluwe–Umfolozi Park, St Lucia Wilderness Area, the Mkhuze Game Reserve and the Drakensberg mountains, including a horseback trail around Giant's Castle.

Fishing

In the Drakensberg region trout and bass fishing is popular at well-stocked dams and streams. The coastline region has many spots for anglers and deep-sea game fishing opportunities are plentiful.

Horse Riding

Visitors can enjoy the experience of seeing the region on horseback. Many of the Drakensberg resorts offer riding trails, as do some of the game reserves.

Diving

Organised dive charters and eco-diving expeditions, focusing on adventure diving and speciality courses exist in areas such as Durban, Aliwal Shoal and Sodwana. Scuba diving courses are available from beginner to instructor level and equipment is available on site.

Golf

Golf is a popular pastime throughout the province. An 18-hole course is to be found at Champagne Sports Resort and nine-hole courses are provided at Champagne Valley, Hlalanathi and Cathedral Peak in the resorts of the Drakensberg mountain range. There are also fine courses at several coastal resorts, such as Sibaya and the Royal Durban Golf Club.

Mountain Biking

Many of the resorts of the Drakensberg offer mountain biking trails, including The Nest, Cathedral Peak Hotel, the Mont-aux-Sources area and Champagne Cottages.

Conservation and Eco-Tourism

The region has several important wildlife conservation areas. Included is the Hluhluwe–Umfolozi Park whose work with the white rhino helped save the species from extinction. Also of note is the conservation work being carried out on the coral reefs and surrounding area of the St Lucia estuary and Lake St Lucia, which is in the throes of being declared a National Heritage Site.

One of the province's finest examples of successful eco-tourism is Conservation Corporation Africa's Phinda Private Game Reserve. The land upon which the reserve is situated was farmland previously utilised for cattle, generating around R75 per hectare per annum. Today, under the new system the same land generates R1 600 per hectare per annum.

The reserve itself employs many people from the local community and has assisted in setting up various small-business developments within the region. It has been instrumental in building schools, crèche facilities and a clinic to serve the region, and in providing wells to make water more accessible – women previously had to travel long distances to carry water.

The reserve has recently received the British Airways World Tourism for Tomorrow Award for the Southern Hemisphere and has been declared a National Heritage Site.

Wildlife Parks and Nature Reserves

There are numerous game and nature reserves throughout KwaZulu-Natal, covering several types of habitat and ecosystems. Accommodation and facilities vary from upmarket bush lodges to camping and caravan facilities. Many have conference facilities, hiking/wilderness trails as well as a host of leisure and sport activities. Specific information on the various reserves may be obtained through the KwaZulu-Natal Nature Conservation Service or local information offices and tourist offices. A few of the well-known reserves are mentioned in detail below.

South Coast

Umtamvuna Nature Reserve

Located on KwaZulu-Natal's south coast, some 8km to the north of Port Edward, is the Umtamvuna Nature Reserve. Established in 1971 along the river, from which it takes its name, the reserve has a wealth of indigenous flora. Conservation projects within the reserve have helped rare and unique plant life re-establish itself in the area. The Oribi antelope, reintroduced to the reserve, are to be seen along with bushbuck, duiker and Cape clawless otters.

Oribi Gorge and Oribi Gorge Nature Reserve

Situated some 20km inland from Port Shepstone on the South Coast, the 24km Oribi Gorge is one of the region's most spectacular gorges which channels water from high in the Drakensberg down to the Indian Ocean. The sandstone cliffs of the gorge, which are covered in dense vegetation, are home to an abundance of indigenous bird life.

The Oribi Gorge Nature Reserve covers an area of some 1 850ha and offers visitors a chance to enjoy the natural wealth of this protected area. The park has a small rest camp that consists of six thatched chalets, a guest cottage, laundry, curio shop, swimming pool and boma. There are also several walking trails traversing the gorge, varying in length from 1,5km to 9km and all clearly marked.

Zululand

Hluhluwe-Umfolozi Park

The 96 000ha Hluhluwe–Umfolozi Park is made up of three reserves: the Hluhluwe and Umfolozi, (both founded in 1895) and the linking Corridor Reserve, proclaimed in 1989. The park is well known for its conservation work and hosts a large variety of wildlife including Africa's Big Five (buffalo, lion, elephant, rhinoceros, leopard), cheetah and wild dog, and has the world's largest population of southern white rhino. The park is criss-crossed with many small tributaries of the Hluhluwe, Black and White Umfolozi rivers and is home to more than 300 species of bird. Facilities available include auto trails, where visitors may discover the bushveld from their own vehicle; self-guided trails; wilderness trails, accompanied by an experienced game ranger, that explore the different aspects of the park's bush life; night drives; day walks; as well as picnic sites. There are several camps to choose from, each varying in style and type of amenities.

Greater St Lucia Wetland Park

The Greater St Lucia Wetland Park stretches along the coast from Mapelane in the south to Sodwana in the north. The area boasts five different ecosystems, endless stretches of spectacular scenery and an immense wealth of animal and bird life. There are several camps located within the park, including the False Bay Park, Cape Vidal and Charters Creek. Facilities include walking trails, boating and fishing as well as a variety of accommodation options catering for all preferences.

Zulu Nyala Game Reserve

Set in a beautiful hilltop location at the foothills of the Lebombo Mountains in Zululand, is the 1 500ha Zulu Nyala Game Reserve. Well stocked with game such as elephant, rhino, buffalo and cheetah, as well as several species of antelope and an abundance of bird life, the reserve's compact size offers visitors with time restrictions a good chance of seeing plenty of game. The park's lodge offers its guests superb accommodation, fine dining and plenty of activities, including river cruises, tennis, horse riding and trips to the nearby Zulu village. Game viewing options include open vehicles, horse or walking trails, all with qualified rangers.

Maputaland

Mkhuze Game Reserve

The 40 000ha Mkhuze Game Reserve was proclaimed a protected area in 1912. It is located to the north west of the Greater St Lucia Wetland Park on the Maputaland coastal plain, some 335km north of Durban. Within the reserve are two beautiful pans, Nhlonhela and Nsumo, home to hippo, crocodile and a large variety of aquatic birds. The park is also known for the sand forest located in the heart of the reserve and a fig forest on the banks of the Nsumo Pan. Facilities include 100km of game viewing roads, picnic spots, conducted game and bird walks, game drives, night drives, wilderness trails and a self-guided trail through the fig forest. Accommodation within the park includes tented safari camps, bush lodges, caravan and camp sites, as well as tented bush lodges with their own cook/camp attendant and field ranger.

A cultural village has been established nearby which sells traditional crafts and offers visitors a glimpse of the traditional lifestyle of the local people.

Sodwana Bay National Park

The park is one of the most popular regions in the greater St Lucia area. The bay has beautiful clear blue waters and offshore coral reefs that attract scuba divers and snorkellers and the abundance of blue and black marlin and tuna attract the deep-sea fisherman to its shores. Loggerhead and leatherback turtles come ashore to nest during the summer and nightly 'turtle tours' are run during December and January for camp residents. There are two self-guided trails that commence close to the camp itself.

Kosi Bay Nature Reserve

The reserve comprises a network of four freshwater lakes extending along the northern Maputaland shoreline, separated from the ocean by high, forested dunes. There is an abundance of fish and birds as well as crocodile, hippo and small antelope, which makes the reserve a popular venue for fishermen, boating enthusiasts and bird-watchers. Accommodation is available in the Kosi Bay Restcamp as well as at campsites.

Phinda Private Game Reserve

The Phinda Private Game Reserve covers an area of some 17 000ha in Maputaland. It is an immense area of fascinating ecological diversity covering seven distinct ecosystems. Luxury accommodation is set in beautiful surroundings, with superb cuisine and personalised service.

Tembe Elephant Park

Lying on the border with Mozambique, the Tembe Elephant Park was established in 1983 to protect the elephants in the area. The region's terrain is fairly impenetrable, consisting of closed thicket, sand forest and the Muzi Swamp, making access to the park limited to four-wheel-drive vehicles. There is a hide overlooking the pan from where one is most likely to spot the elusive elephants. Two walking trails are available but only one party of visitors is allowed into the park daily, accompanied by a park ranger. There are picnic spots and accommodation is provided for a maximum of eight in a tented camp.

Drakensberg

Royal Natal National Park

The Royal Natal National Park, situated in the Drakensberg mountains, offers its visitors a wide range of walking and riding paths amidst some of the region's most magnificent mountain scenery. The park has a wide range of tourist facilities and accommodation options. Forming the spectacular backdrop to the Park are the 1 000m basalt cliffs of the Amphitheatre which stretch some 4km between the Eastern Buttress and the Sentinel.

Tourist Attractions

The Coastal Regions

Durban

The city of Durban has much to offer its visitors and is one of the nation's premier tourist destinations. The city itself has a host of interesting sights, markets and shopping malls as well as some fine architecture. The hub of Durban's historic centre is the City Hall, which houses a natural science museum and an art gallery. Completed in 1910, the ornate building is a replica of the one in Belfast, Northern Ireland. Other places of interest include those listed below.

Golden Mile

▶ The Sea World Aquarium and Dolphinarium

▶ Fitzsimon's Snake Park

▶ Minitown

▶ Waterworld

▶ The ricksha pullers

▷ *Colourful ricksha pullers*

▷ *The Durban seafront*

Museums and Landmarks

Within the City Centre:

- ▶ The City Hall
- ▶ Natural Science Museum
- ▶ Local History Museum

The Victoria Embankment:

- ▶ Port Natal Maritime Museum
- ▶ Da Gama Clock
- ▶ Dick King Statue
- ▶ The Harbour

Indian District

- ▶ Victoria Street Market
- ▶ The Madressa Arcade
- ▶ Jumma Mosque

South Coast

The coastline extending southwards from Durban to Port Edward and the Eastern Cape border has long been a favourite holiday playground for residents of Gauteng and Free State. The area offers a wide range of accommodation, sporting facilities, nature reserves and tourist attractions set amongst a beautiful, fertile subtropical landscape. Long stretches of golden, sandy beaches are lapped by the warm waters of the Indian Ocean. Popular resorts include, among others, Amanzimtoti, Scottburgh, Port Shepstone, Uvongo, Margate, Ramsgate and Port Edward. Main attractions along the coastline include diving sites at Aliwal Shoal and the Protea Banks at Shelley Beach, the Oribi Gorge and Umtamvuna Nature Reserves and the Banana Express Steam Train which runs daily trips from Port Shepstone to Paddock.

▷ *South Coast beach scene*

Tourism Destinations Southern Africa

North Coast

The region between Umhlanga and the Tugela Mouth is known as the Dolphin Coast. The old coastal route follows this long stretch of tropical coastline passing through the popular holiday resorts of Umhlanga Rocks, Umhloti, Ballito and Salt

Rock, which boast idyllic holiday homes, hotel complexes, superb golf courses and a wealth of recreational activities.

Sun International's Zimbali Lodge is located within the region, offering guests five-star luxury accommodation set in exquisite surroundings of lush tropical forests. Amenities at the adjacent Zimbali Country Club include an 18-hole golf course, and tennis courts.

▷ *Sun International's Zimbali Lodge*

Umhlanga Rocks

A favourite holiday destination along the northern coastline is Umhlanga Rocks. The offices of the Natal Sharks Board are situated here, on the hill behind the town. The centre studies the lifecycle of the shark and offers tours that include shark dissection. The resort has two interesting wreck dives and there are several small nature reserves located within the area.

Salt Rock and Shaka's Rock

Salt Rock takes its name from the rock where the Zulus used to collect salt. Close by is Shaka's Rock, a cliff from which Shaka is believed to have thrown his enemies.

Zululand

The region known as Zululand begins on the northern bank of the Tugela River and continues along the coastline as far as Maputaland, extending inland to Mkuze, Vryheid, Paulpietersburg and up to the Swaziland border.

The climate of the region is hot and humid along the coastal belt with sea breezes sweeping in over the higher ground, cooling the air and bringing rain. Summer is hot, with rain falling most afternoons, whereas winters tend to be mild and dry.

The region has much to offer visitors by way of scenic beauty, culture and history. It is the home of the Zulu nation and has numerous historic sites and battlefields dating from the Anglo–Zulu and Anglo–Boer Wars.

The province's main game reserves of Hluhluwe–Umfolozi and St. Lucia are situated here. There is a wide variety of handicraft centres that attract visitors, and recreational facilities include numerous hiking trails, deep-sea fishing, scuba diving and water sport opportunities.

Greater St Lucia Wetland Park Region

The Greater St Lucia Wetland Park region boasts countless water sport amenities, superb game fishing and a host of hiking and walking trails. There is a wide range of accommodation facilities varying from guesthouse, self-catering and camp and caravan sites.

Ulundi – The Valley of the Kings

Ulundi was originally known as Ondini and was established by the Zulu king Cetshwayo in 1873. It is the legislative capital of KwaZulu-Natal and has a rich and colourful history. Its legislative complex has an excellent display of tapestries depicting historical events of the region. Accommodation in the area ranges from modern hotels to traditional kraals.

The nearby Ondini Cultural History Museum, built on the site of Cetshwayo's Royal Kraal, affords visitors an understanding of the history of the Zulu nation.

Eshowe

Once the home of Zulu Kings Shaka, Mpande, Cetshwayo and Dinizulu and the first British capital of Zululand, the town of Eshowe is steeped in history, which is depicted in the Zululand Historical Museum housed at Fort Nongqayi.

Shakaland

Situated some 13km north of Eshowe, Shakaland is a popular Zulu village offering tours where customs are explained, dancing is performed and a traditional lunch is served.

Maputaland

Maputaland is a fairly underdeveloped region of the province, covering an area of some 9 000 sq km from Lake St Lucia to the Mozambique border and inland to the Lebombo mountains. It has a large diversity of ecosystems ranging from the coastal plains to the forests of the Lebombo Mountains. South Africa's largest freshwater lake, Lake Sibaya, is located here. Large expanses of the land are protected areas and there is a wealth of bird life, flora and fauna.

Pietermaritzburg and the Natal Midlands

The Natal Midlands is a region of rolling green hills and valleys. Small country villages and art and craft studios abound, as do bed and breakfast establishments, guesthouses and beautiful country hotels.

Pietermaritzburg

Pietermaritzburg is the joint capital of the province with Ulundi. It was named after the Voortrekker leaders Gert Maritz and Piet Retief who settled in the area in 1838. Much of its architecture dates to the time when the city was the capital of the Colony of Natal and it retains much of its colonial atmosphere and charm. Places of interest include City Hall, Memorial Arch, Zulu War Memorial, Statue of Ghandi, Macrorie House, Natal Museum, and the Voortrekker Museum. The city's publicity association provides information on a self-guided town trail that takes you through the city's historical centre.

The city is the focal point for two of the country's most popular sporting events: the internationally patronised Comrades Marathon run between Durban and Pietermaritzburg; and the Duzi Canoe Marathon (on the Msunduze River), the oldest race of its kind in Africa.

Midlands Meander

The Midlands Meander is an art and craft route that stretches from Hilton to Mooi River and from the Dargle Valley in the west to Rietvlei in the east. The route, which is open daily, originated during the mid-1980s when a few painters, potters and weavers opened their studios and workshops to the public. Today the route has grown to be the largest of its kind in South Africa.

Battlefield Route

The northern and central region of KwaZulu-Natal boasts the largest concentration of battlefields in South Africa. It was in this region that much of the nation's turbulent history took place and several military memorials in and around the towns of Ladysmith, Utrecht, Ulundi, Dundee and Vryheid, commemorate the battles fought during the Voortrekker–Zulu, Anglo–Zulu and Anglo–Boer wars. Some of the most famous sites include:

Umgungundhlovu

Umgungundhlovu (place of the big elephant) was the royal town of the 19th century Zulu king Dingaan and the site where Piet Retief and his men died at the hand of Dingaan in 1838. Of further interest is the fact that Natal's former colonial capital of Pietermaritzburg first had the name Umgungundhlovu attributed to it by the Zulu people.

Blood River

A stone memorial and bronze replica of the Voortrekker Laager (circle of wagons) are to be found at the site where the Battle of Blood River took place on 16 December 1838.

Isandhlwana

A monument marks the site of the first battle of the Anglo–Zulu War at Isandhlwana which took place on 22 January 1879.

Rorke's Drift

An important battlefield during the Anglo–Zulu War.

Majuba

Site of the battle on 27 Feburary 1881 between Boer and British forces.

Vryheid

The area around Vryheid has a wealth of historical battle sites from the Anglo–Zulu and Anglo–Boer wars. Famous battles such as Scheepersnek, Blood River Poort,

Holkrans, Hlobane and Kambula were fought not far from the town. The Nieuwe Republiek Museum, the Old Carnegie Library and the Residence of President Lucas Meijer are three museums situated in the town which portray interesting relics of its past.

Spioenkop

An important site of the Anglo–Boer War when in January 1900 a battle fought between Boer and Briton saw over 2 000 troops killed.

Drakensberg

The Drakensberg is a region of captivating beauty, with an abundance of flora and fauna and numerous species of bird. Several resorts have been established within the area with accommodation options ranging from 5-star luxury to camp and caravan sites. Popular venues include the Royal Natal National Park, Mont-aux-Sources, the Cathedral Peak Hotel, Champagne Castle and the Drakensberg Sun. Facilities also exist for a host of sport activities, including day walks and hiking, horse trails, mountain bike riding, fishing and golf.

There are several art and craft centres selling locally made handicrafts. A good example is Thandanani Craft Village situated close to the Royal Natal National Park.

The world-renowned Drakensberg Boys' Choir school is located close to the Dragon Peaks Park. The choir consists of boys with music and singing ability, and aged between nine and fifteen. Concerts are held in the school auditorium every Wednesday during school terms.

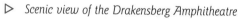

▷ *Scenic view of the Drakensberg Amphitheatre*

San Rock Art

The Drakensberg region is famous for its San rock paintings and sites are to be found throughout the area. The most popular and easily accessible is in the Giant's Castle area where the Main Caves Museum depicts the daily life of a hunter-gatherer family.

Cultural Villages

Kwabhekithunga – Stewarts Farm

Kwabhekithunga, the tribal home of Mbhangcuza (Thomas) Fakude and his family, lies just off the R34. The (Umazi) Zulu village welcomes visitors and offers them an opportunity to experience Zulu culture and traditions, as well as an elaborate meal prepared the Zulu way. The village has a handicraft centre selling goods made by the families living in the area. Overnight accommodation is available in traditional Zulu 'beehive' huts each fitted with showers and toilets en suite. Facilities include a swimming pool, licensed bar and hiking trails.

▷ *Zulu village life*

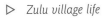

Activity

Detail the location and the activities available in the following wildlife reserves:

Hluhluwe–Umfolozi Park, Mkhuze, Greater St Lucia Wetland Park, Kosi Bay Nature Reserve, Phinda Private Game Reserve, Tembe Elephant Park, Sodwana Bay National Park.

WESTERN CAPE

Facts at a Glance

Capital	Cape Town
Size	129 370 sq km
Population	3,96m
Average Temperature	Summer min 16°C/max 26°C
– Cape Town	Winter min 8°C/max 18°C
Main Languages	English, Afrikaans, isiXhosa

Geographical Outline

Situated at the south-western tip of the African continent, Western Cape is bordered by Northern Cape and Eastern Cape. The southern shores are washed by the Indian Ocean, which is warmed by the strong Mozambique current, and the Atlantic Ocean, with its cold Benguela Current, is on the western seaboard.

Apart from the majesty of the Table Mountain chain in the Mother City of Cape Town, famous throughout the world, there are numerous other spectacular mountain ranges in the province. Numbered among them are the Outeniekwaberge and Swartberg along the Garden Route, Langeberg and Riviersonderend mountains in the south, the Nuweveldberge in the north, and the Cederberg in the northwest. The Olifants, Berg, Breede and Eerste rivers are the major rivers flowing through Western Cape.

The terrain of the province varies dramatically from one region to another. The starkly beautiful surrounds of the West Coast lead inland to the vast wheat lands and sheep farming area of the Swartland (Malmesbury and beyond). Vineyards of the rich and fertile Winelands extend through the Little Karoo, Paarl, Robertson, Stellenbosch, the Swartland, Tulbagh, Walker Bay and Worcester. The semi-arid Karoo has its own mystique with its dry sweeping plains where conditions are generally hot and dry and vegetation somewhat sparse. In contrast to this, forests, deep valleys, breathtaking mountain passes, rivers and waterfalls abound along the Garden Route and include the lake district and lagoons around Knysna and the Wilderness. The terrain in the Overberg district ranges from forests to green pastures and wheat and barley fields.

The Cape Floral Kingdom extends along the south-western and southern coast and includes nearly 8 600 different flora species – the richest concentration in the world. The number of species in the Cape of Good Hope Nature Reserve alone exceeds that of the whole of Great Britain. Known collectively as *fynbos*, the flora mainly comprises low-growing evergreen shrubs and numerous species of erica and protea, including South Africa's national flower, the King Protea.

Introduction

The Region

The province of Western Cape is considered to be one of the country's most beautiful regions, graced with spectacular mountains, verdant green valleys, scenic coastlines and endless stretches of beach. Against the backdrop of this magnificent setting, the area has much to offer in the form of eco-tourism, cultural heritage, history and adventure.

▷ *The King Protea – South Africa's national flower*

The Economy

Important economic sectors in Western Cape are tourism, agriculture, mining, forestry, shipping (imports and exports), fishing and manufacturing. It is expected that economic growth in the region will continue to exceed national levels.

The Importance of Tourism

Cape Town has risen to become the third most popular tourist destination in the world and, consequently, tourism is one of the biggest contributors to the economy of Western Cape with some 1,1 million local and foreign tourists visiting the region annually.

Climate

The climate of the province is mostly Mediterranean, with warm dry summers and mild wet winters during which snow occasionally falls on the mountains of the Boland and the Cederberg. The hot, dry 'berg winds', which blow in from the north-west, sometimes bring unseasonable warm sunny spells during the winter, but they also usually herald rain. The forceful south-easterly wind known as the 'Cape Doctor' is common during the summer when it can reach gale-force, particularly across the Cape Peninsula.

An exception to the typical weather patterns of the province is the Karoo, where winters are dry, little rain falls during the summer and temperatures are generally higher than in the coastal regions. The Garden Route experiences a temperate climate, with warm summers and mild winters and rain throughout the year.

Transportation and Accessibility

Road

Situated some 1 402km from Johannesburg, the city has an excellent network of national highways and secondary roads which connect all the major cities. The N1 links Cape Town with Beaufort West, Bloemfontein, Johannesburg, Pretoria, Pietersburg and the Beit Bridge border post with Zimbabwe. The N2 takes the southerly route along the coastline from Cape Town to Knysna, Port Elizabeth, Grahamstown, East London, Umtata, Durban and on to the northern coastline of KwaZulu-Natal before turning inland towards Mpumalanga. The N7 turns northwards and follows the western coast, connecting with Springbok in Northern Cape and the Namibian border. Several dramatic passes cut through the Cape mountains from the coast to the interior.

Inter-city buses connect Cape Town with all the main cities of the country and regional bus services and car hire companies operate in major centres throughout the province.

Air

Cape Town International Airport is served by several international airlines as well as by domestic and regional carriers. Domestic airports are situated at George, Plettenberg Bay, Oudtshoorn and Alexander Bay.

Rail

Many mainline trains operate within Western Cape. The area also boasts an extensive regional and urban rail network. The world famous Blue Train and Rovos Rail–Pride of Africa offer luxury rail transportation between Cape Town and Pretoria and the steam train, the Outeniqua Tjoe-Choo, runs between George and Knysna.

Accommodation

The entire province offers an immense choice of accommodation to suit all needs and every budget. Hotels, guesthouses and lodges, as well as bed and breakfast, self-catering and caravan and camping facilities are to be found throughout the region. Advance booking is advised at peak periods especially in summer during the December–January school holidays.

Historic Highlights

The Khoikhoi and San were the first inhabitants of the region.

In 1652 the Dutch East India Company, under the leadership of Jan van Riebeeck, landed at Table Bay with instructions to establish a refreshment station, or halfway-house, for their ships to replenish stocks of fresh food and water. A mud-walled fortress was built and fruit and vegetable gardens were laid out so that provisions were soon available to ships on their trade route between Europe and the Far East. The Castle was built between 1666 and 1679 to replace the original fort.

In 1657, in and attempt to make the settlement self-supporting, permission was given to release nine married men from their company's services in order for them to become farmers. Known as 'free burghers', they would be free from paying taxes for the first twelve years but would have to agree to remain in the country for twenty years. This act was to change the refreshment station to a colony as the Cape settlement grew.

In 1688 a group of French Huguenots, fleeing religious persecution in Europe, settled along the Drakenstein Valley of the Cape.

In 1795 the British took over the Cape of Good Hope from the Dutch. The colony briefly returned to Dutch rule between 1803–1806 and thereafter remained a British Colony until 1910.

Population

Traditionally, the population mix of the province has been English- Afrikaans- and Xhosa-speaking communities. However, in recent years Cape Town has attracted people from all corners of the world and is today a truly cosmopolitan metropolis.

Social and Cultural Profile

In Cape Town these numerous cultures have blended together to create the unique character of the city and its suburban surroundings. Art and culture thrive alongside sport and recreation and several theatre complexes provide opera, ballet, drama and musicals. The Cape Town Philharmonic Orchestra can be heard in the City Hall and various other forms of live entertainment can be enjoyed in the city's numerous night spots.

Sport and Leisure Facilities

The Cape's beauty and diversity make it a favourite venue for a wide variety of sport and leisure activities. There are numerous hiking possibilities, adventure sport venues and all types of water sport are catered for along the coastline and on rivers and dams. Spectator sports may be enjoyed at venues such as the renowned cricket grounds and rugby stadium of Newlands, the Green Point Stadium that hosts athletic meetings and various other events, the main soccer stadium at Hartleyvale, and Kenilworth Park where horseracing meetings are held.

Popular adventure sports include rock climbing, bungee jumping, paragliding, mountain biking, 4 x 4 trails, river rafting and canoeing.

Water sports include deep-sea diving, water-skiing, windsurfing, surfing and yachting and there are many angling sites and opportunities for big game fishing. Facilities also exist for golf, squash and tennis and there is a varied choice of health clubs and swimming pools.

Hiking

Hiking trails abound and detailed information can be obtained at tourist information offices throughout the province. Some of the better-known trails include the 108km, 7-day Outeniqua Hiking Trail which starts at the Old Forest Station at Beervlei and ends at the Harkerville Forestry Station; the 24km Vineyard Trail between Stellenbosch and Kuils River; and trails along the Garden Route and in the Cederberg Wilderness Area.

Fishing

Fishing is a major sporting activity along Western Cape's coastline and in its rivers and dams. Information on the wide variety of fishing possibilities is available at local tourism offices.

Cycling

Several outlets hire out bicycles and will provide information on the best cycling routes available. Cycling has an enthusiastic following and the annual cycle race around the peninsula, sponsored by The Argus/Pick 'n Pay, attracts local and foreign entrants.

Diving

Various diving centres exist along the Cape coastline offering equipment hire, boat charters and diving courses.

Canoeing

Canoeing is a popular pastime in the region. Venues include the overnight canoeing trail at the Keurbooms River Nature Reserve and the Wine Route Canoe Adventures on the Breede River.

Conservation and Eco-Tourism

The Western Cape's wildlife parks and nature reserves play a vital role in conservation, providing a safe haven for numerous species of mammals, marine and bird life, such as the jackass penguin found only in a few areas along the coast of South Africa. These fragile ecosystems are closely monitored and protected from factors such as pollution and human encroachment.

▷ *Jackass penguins are found in only a few areas along the South African coast*

Wildlife Parks and Nature Reserves

Cape of Good Hope Nature Reserve

Situated some 70km from Cape Town's city centre, the 7 750ha nature reserve is one of the main tourist attractions of the region and includes the famous landmark, Cape Point.

There is an abundance of indigenous flora, fauna and bird life. Hartmann's mountain zebra, eland, baboon, porcupine, springbok and bontebok live in the reserve. Of the variety of birds to be seen is the ostrich and fish eagle, and on the beaches the oyster-catcher.

The reserve has a good network of roads, several walks, beaches, picnic spots and braai (barbecue) facilities, as well as a gift shop and a restaurant offering spectacular views across False Bay.

Wilderness National Park

The Wilderness National Park is situated on either side of the N2 highway between Wilderness and Knysna. The park covers an area of some 2 500ha, adjoining some 10 000ha of conservation land. Within these confines are five lakes, two estuaries and almost 30km of shoreline, as well as the wooded slopes below the Outeniqua Mountains. The park offers a choice of accommodation and leisure facilities that include water sport, angling and hiking possibilities.

Knysna (Lagoon) National Lakes Area

The Knysna National Lakes Area represents over 15 000ha of the Knysna Lagoon and is protected by the National Parks Board. The area is home to a large variety of both marine and bird life. The Featherbed Nature Reserve, situated on the Western Head of Knysna, provides a sanctuary for the endangered blue duiker. Also situated within the reserve is a cave once inhabited by Khoikhoi (*Strandlopers*).

West Coast National Park

The West Coast National Park was established in 1985 to protect the marine life in the Langebaan Lagoon and coastal wetlands. The park is rich in bird life, has several head of small antelope, and fields carpeted with wildflowers that bloom after the first spring rains.

Bontebok National Park

Situated some 7km from the town of Swellendam is the 2 800ha Bontebok National Park. The original reserve was established in the Bredasdorp area in 1931 to save the bontebok from extinction. Thirty years later the park was moved to its present location beside the Breede River where it provides a sanctuary for around 200 bontebok, various other species of antelope and the Cape mountain zebra. It is also known for its abundant bird life and floral wealth. Viewing can be enjoyed along the park's 25km of roads or on two short walking trails. The park has an information centre, shop, picnic and braai areas, as well as a caravan and camp site.

Karoo National Park

The Karoo National Park is situated close to the N1 highway approximately 10km north of the town of Beaufort West. It was created to conserve a small portion of the unique Karoo environment. The 32 792ha park, proclaimed in 1979, is home to a large variety of wildlife and over 174 bird species. There is a 27km, 3-day, circular Springbok Hiking Trail, which starts from the park's rest camp, as well as three short day-walks. Self-contained chalet accommodation is available at the main rest camp, basic huts at the Mountain View rest camp, and a camp and caravan site. Other facilities include a restaurant, a curio shop, two information centres, and picnic spots. The park provides game viewing opportunities, a 4 x 4 trail and night drives under the guidance of trained staff. This is an ideal stopover on the N1 route.

Tourist Attractions

Cape Town

"The fairest cape we saw in the whole circumference of the earth" – words of the early navigator Sir Francis Drake, on first rounding the Cape in 1577. The province's capital city, Cape Town, also known as the Mother City and Tavern of the Seas, is considered to be one of the world's most beautiful cities.

Cape Town has much that is of historic and cultural interest in its many museums and buildings, as well as a wide variety of shopping facilities ranging from upmarket shopping malls to roadside stalls and flea markets. There are several white-sand beaches nearby, offering safe bathing, water sport and angling facilities. Restaurants, pubs, theatres and cinemas provide a wide range of culinary delights and entertainment.

A burgeoning aspect of tourism is organised township tours that take in visits to popular nightspots and shebeens and there are also bed and breakfast facilities available.

Favourite tourist venues among the many options available within the city limits, are considered below.

Table Mountain

Cape Town's most famous landmark and one of its main tourist attractions, Table Mountain rises some 1 086m above the bay and is an impressive spectacle from land, sea or air. The mountaintop is accessible by cable car or by way of numerous climbing paths, although caution is advised especially in bad weather. The mountain is a World Heritage Site. In 1999 the entire mountain chain, from Table Mountain to Cape Point, was proclaimed a reserve – The Cape Peninsula National Park – in order to protect and preserve the environs.

The slopes and central plateau host a large variety of the indigenous flora of the region, including the silver tree and red disa, fondly known as the Pride of Table Mountain. There is a restaurant and souvenir shop situated at the summit.

▷ *Table Mountain is Cape Town's most famous landmark and one of its main tourist attractions*

Victoria and Alfred Waterfront

Situated at Table Bay Harbour, the Victoria and Alfred Waterfront development has become one of Cape Town's most popular tourist venues. The complex offers hotels, restaurants, theatres, cinemas, speciality shops and arts and crafts, as well as places of interest such as the SA Maritime Museum, Two Oceans Aquarium and a tour of a ship at its moorings, the SAS Somerset. Tours of the harbour are on offer in a variety of vessels.

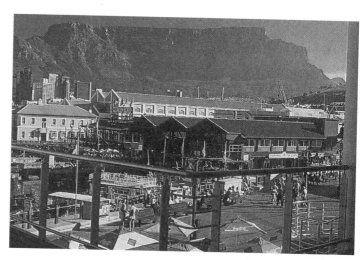

▷ *The Victoria and Alfred Waterfront development has become one of Cape Town's top tourist attractions*

Robben Island

Robben Island has become one of the Cape's most popular tourist attractions. It is a national monument and important historic site with a chequered history. The island gained notoriety as the jail that housed Nelson Mandela. Tours of the island and museum are popular and ferry bookings must be made in advance.

Castle of Good Hope and Military Museum

The Castle was built between 1666 and 1679 and is one of the city's oldest buildings and most prominent landmarks. Today it is still used as the regional offices of the National Defence Force. Three museums are housed within the castle – part of the William Fehr Collection, which displays pictorial Africana and antique furnishings; Secunde's House, which recreates the living conditions of officials of the Dutch East India Company during the 17th and 18th century; and the Military Museum portraying the military history of the Castle. Guided tours operate throughout the day, and a full ceremonial Changing of the Guard takes place at noon.

The Company Gardens

The gardens were originally established to provide fresh produce for the passing ships. Buildings housed within the original 18ha of gardens included a pleasure lodge which was rebuilt and is now known as Tuynhuys, the residence of South Africa's State President; and a Slave Lodge, which is now the Cultural History Museum. Today the gardens have been reduced to about 6ha but still boast 3 000 different species of flora.

Houses of Parliament

Situated in Parliament Street, the building dates back to 1885 and became the seat of the national parliament when the Union of South Africa was formed in 1910. Gallery tickets are available when parliament is in session and guided tours of the chambers and Constitutional Assembly are available during the recess period.

City Hall

The City Hall was completed in 1905 and overlooks the Grand Parade. It accommodates the Cape Town Philharmonic Orchestra and the City Library. The municipal carillon located in the tower dates back to 1923 and contains thirty-nine bells.

South African Museum

Founded by Governor Lord Charles Somerset in 1825, the museum has numerous exhibits including that of the history, art and lifestyle of the San people, and the Whale Well which contains plaster casts of some of the world's largest mammals.

Groot Constantia

Groot Constantia is one of the most famous of the Cape's historic homes. The house was designed and built by the Cape Governor, Simon van der Stel, who lived in the house between 1699 until his death in 1712. The Cape–Dutch style farmstead is now a national monument and has been restored after a fire destroyed the building in 1925. The estate has two excellent restaurants – the Jonkershuis, which serves traditional Cape lunches and teas, and the Tavern, which serves buffet meals.

Kirstenbosch National Botanical Gardens

Kirstenbosch Botanical Gardens was proclaimed as a National Botanical Garden in 1913 and is the oldest and largest of its kind in South Africa. The original farmland, bought in 1895 by Cecil John Rhodes, was bequeathed to the nation. Of particular interest are the Braille Trail, the Conservatory, the Fragrance Garden, Herb Garden and Van Riebeeck's Hedge, a portion of the hedge of wild almond trees planted in 1660 by Jan van Riebeeck as part of the physical boundary of the first Dutch settlement. The Skeleton Path, or Smut's Trail, starts in the gardens and follows the stream through the forest and up to the summit of Table Mountain.

Newlands

Situated on the back slopes of Table Mountain, Newlands is best known for its cricket ground, and as the home of the Western Province Rugby Union. Places of interest include Josephine Mill, situated near the entrance to the rugby stadium, and the South African Rugby Museum, where the history of South African rugby is exhibited along with a wealth of memorabilia and photographs.

Bo Kaap and the Bo-Kaap Museum

The erstwhile Malay Quarter of the city, Bo Kaap is situated on the slopes of Signal Hill. Many of its flat-roofed houses date back to the late 18th and early 19th century. The cosmopolitan mix of residents includes a large Islamic community whose forebears were brought to the Cape as slaves or exiles by the Dutch East India Company, from the islands of the East. The Bo-Kaap Museum portrays much of the cultural heritage of the Cape Malay people.

Signal Hill

The Noon Gun on top of Signal Hill is fired every day at noon, except Sunday. The gun was originally used to signal the correct time to the ships in Table Bay.

Ratanga Junction

Located to the north of the city is Cape Town's first full-scale entertainment complex, Ratanga Junction. The 20ha African theme park has more than 30 attractions, including roller coaster rides, jungle cruises and variety shows, as well as theme restaurants and live entertainment.

Cape Peninsula

The Cape Peninsula extends into the sea at the extreme south-western corner of the province. At its most southerly tip lies the Cape of Good Hope Nature Reserve and Cape Point. It is one of the Cape's main tourist attractions and a popular day trip from Cape Town.

Surrounded by almost 150km of coastline, the Peninsula is a favourite area among beach lovers for swimming, fishing and a host of water sport activities. There are also numerous historic sites and hiking trails in the area.

Cape Point

Cape Point offers superb views over the cliffs and out across the ocean. Dolphins, seals and whales are often sighted from the viewpoint, which can be reached by way of a fairly steep walk or funicular.

Sea Point

The popular seaside suburb of Sea Point has numerous hotels, delicatessens, restaurants and night spots.

Clifton Beach

Clifton Beach is an upmarket, popular area considered by many to be the place to be seen. It has four broad white sand beaches which are sheltered from the wind by the rock formation known as Lion's Head.

Camps Bay

Beneath the slopes of the Twelve Apostles lies the white-sand beach of Camps Bay, which has a permanent holiday atmosphere. It is one of Cape Town's most frequented beaches.

Hout Bay

The picturesque village and fishing harbour at Hout Bay is another of the region's popular tourist venues. The busy harbour is full of yachts and fishing boats, and fish is sold on the quayside. The Mariner's Wharf complex, situated at the quayside, has a seafood restaurant and bistro, a fresh fish outlet and marine-orientated gift shop. Tourist attractions within the area include the Hout Bay Museum, which details the natural and cultural history of the area; the World of Birds, South Africa's largest bird park with over 100 aviaries built to simulate the birds' natural habitat; and Kronendal, a Cape–Dutch H-plan homestead built in 1800 that has been declared a national monument and houses a fine restaurant.

Simon's Town

Simon's Town has strong naval ties, which play an important part in the town's atmosphere. A statue of Able Seaman Just Nuisance stands in Jubilee Square in honour of the faithful canine mascot of the Royal Navy during World War 11. The South African Naval Museum is numbered among a number of interesting museums in the town. There are several walking trails, including a guided historical walk on Saturdays, visits to the penguin colony, and boat rides around the harbour and to Cape Point.

Muizenberg

Muizenberg, immortalised in the writings of Rudyard Kipling, has played host to numerous other famous persons including Cecil John Rhodes who spent his last years at Barkly Cottage (now known as Rhodes Cottage, situated between Muizenberg and St. James).

The history of the resort revolves around The Battle of Muizenberg between the Dutch and the British in 1795. Nowadays it is the False Bay paradise for swimmers and surfers and offers a pavilion and an amusement park for the benefit of the many visitors to the area.

Winelands

Located some 30 minutes drive from the centre of Cape Town, the Winelands region offers visitors a breathtakingly beautiful but different vista of this diverse province. It is an area of gracious Cape–Dutch homesteads set among the vineyards in fertile green valleys beneath the Cape mountains. Numerous different wine routes may be explored by car or by way of a guided tour from Cape Town. Apart from the Constantia wine farms and those in the Robertson and Tulbagh regions, the best-known wine routes are those of Stellenbosch, Paarl and Franschhoek. Many of the estates provide luxury accommodation, such as the Eikendal Lodge guesthouse at the Eikendal Estate in Stellenbosch and the 18th century Manor House – La Grande Roche in Paarl.

Stellenbosch and the Stellenbosch Wine Route

Stellenbosch

Picturesque Stellenbosch is South Africa's second oldest town after Cape Town. It was developed by a group of settlers who had been granted land on the banks of the Eerste River. Its educational heritage dates back to 1859 when permission was granted to establish a theological seminary. Today it boasts several educational institutions as well as faithfully restored Cape–Dutch, Georgian, Regency and Victorian buildings, an abundance of hotels, restaurants, cafes, bars and shops.

The many places of interest are best viewed on foot, aided by the brochure, 'Discover Stellenbosch on Foot' which is available at the tourist and information bureau. Popular sites include the Village Museum, the Braak, D'Ouwe Werf, the University, Libertas Parva, the Oude Meester Brandy Museum, the Bergkelder and Oom Samie se Winkel.

There are several sport and leisure activities within the vicinity, including cycling, mountain biking, horse riding, golf, game viewing, walking and hiking trails and spectator sports such as rugby, cricket and athletics. Annual events that take place within the region are the Stellenbosch Festival during September, the Simon van der Stel Festival on the Saturday nearest to the 14th October, and the Food and Wine Festival during the last week of October.

A regular train service runs from Cape Town to Stellenbosch and the journey takes approximately one hour.

Each of the numerous wine farms within the Stellenbosch region has its own particular charm and character:

Blaauwklippen

The Blaauwklippen estate dates back some 300 years and is a fine example of the H-shaped Cape homestead, with thatched roof, gables and a stoep (verandah). In addition to the wine, the estate produces preserves and relishes prepared to original Cape Malay recipes. On offer are wine tasting and sales, cellar tours, lunches and coach rides.

Hazendal

The Hazendal wine estate is one of the oldest and most beautiful estates in the country and its farm is a national monument. Wine tasting, sales, cellar tours and lunches are available for visitors.

Neethlingshof

Neethlingshof is considered to be one of the most appealing wine estates in the area, combining carefully restored historic buildings with up-to-date cellar technology. The estate boasts two restaurants, the notable Lord Neethling, and the Palm Terrace. Wine sales, tasting, cellar tours are offered as well as estate tours during the summer months.

Rust en Vrede

Dating back to 1780, the Rust en Vrede estate offers an opportunity to view the charming Cape–Dutch architecture whilst enjoying the sampling of its wine and viewing of its cellars.

Spier

Spier brings together at one venue the lure of South African history, the charm of the Wine Route and the flavours of a variety of South African foods. Facilities include formal and informal restaurants, an amphitheatre, conference venues, an Equestrian Centre and the excitement of a Cheetah Outreach Breeding Centre. The estate is an exceptional setting for weddings, conferences, product launches and a wide variety of functions.

Representing more than 200 different private estates and eight international estates, regular tastings are offered at The Spier Wine Centre. A range of treats is available at the authentic farm stall and areas have been set aside for picnics. Day-trippers from Cape Town can travel on the Spier Vintage Train, on charter bookings only. Trips are also available on specific dates during the Spier Summer Festival.

Paarl and the Paarl Wine Route

Paarl

The historic town of Paarl was founded in 1720 as a wagon-building and farming centre. Today the town is noted for its fine buildings, jacaranda trees and the oaks lining the main street, which runs some 10km from end to end. The popular Paarl Nouveau Wine Festival is held every April and involves the local winemakers who deliver the season's first products to people waiting on the summit of Paarl Mountain.

The Paarl Wine Route meanders through the Berg River Valley and includes, among others, the famous KWV cellars and internationally famous Nederburg Wine Estate.

KWV (Ko-operatiewe Wijnbouwers-Vereeniging)

KWV is one of the world's largest wine co-operatives. The complex is open to the public on weekdays and offers informative cellar tours and wine tasting.

Nederburg Wine Estate

The Nederburg wine estate has an H-shaped Cape–Dutch homestead and is very well known for its famous wines. The name of Nederburg is immediately associated with the renowned annual wine auction it hosts in April. Wine tasting and sales are open Monday to Saturday. Cellar tours are by appointment only. Picnic lunches are available between 1 November and 1 March.

Franschhoek and the Franschhoek Wine Estates

Franschhoek

The historic town of Franschhoek was founded in 1688 by the French Huguenot refugees. Of special interest is the Huguenot Memorial and adjacent museum complex. The town also boasts several fine French-style restaurants and bistros, and numerous art and craft shops.

Some of the wine estates of the region are not open to the public or open by appointment only. The most well known estates of the region are Boschendal and Bellingham.

▷ *The Huguenot Memorial at Franschhoek*

Boschendal

The majestic Boschendal wine farm is considered by many to be a favourite among the Cape wine estates. The Cape Flemish manor house dates back to 1812 and is now a museum, which has been fully restored and fitted with fine antique furniture. The Taphuis serves as a winery and tasting room and the Waenhuis has been turned into a gift shop. Boschendal has a superb restaurant serving traditional Cape cuisine and, in summertime, offers luncheon picnic baskets on the lawn.

▷ *Summer picnic lunches on the beautiful Boschendal wine estate*

Bellingham

The Bellingham Estate is renowned for its dry white wines. The estate has a natural amphitheatre seating around 90 people, which is periodically used for musical and other performances. Cellar tours, wine tasting and sales as well as light lunches are provided during the summer months.

Garden Route

The Garden Route follows the coast between the town of Mossel Bay and the Storms River and is one of South Africa's most popular tourist destinations. The Outeniqua and Tsitsikamma mountains form a backdrop to the numerous bays and secluded beaches lining the coast. It is a region of lush vegetation and verdant forests encompassing nature reserves and hiking trails, many interesting towns and places of historic interest, as well as a host of sport and leisure facilities.

Tourism Destinations Southern Africa

George

George is principal town of the Garden Route. Situated some 420km from Cape Town and 320km from Port Elizabeth, it has good road, rail and air links to all South Africa's main centres. There are a wide variety of accommodation possibilities, several hiking trails and a choice of sporting facilities including two of the country's best golf courses. Places of historic interest worth visiting include the Drostdy and George Museum and St. Mark's Cathedral. The town is also a starting point for the steam locomotive, the Outeniqua Tjoe-Choo, which travels the scenic route between George and Knysna.

Mossel Bay

The warm coastal waters of Mossel Bay make this a favourite holiday resort. Sporting activities include deep-sea fishing, scuba diving, abseiling, rock climbing and bungee jumping. Places of interest include the Bartolomeu Dias Museum Complex, which contains a replica of the caravel of this intrepid seafarer; exhibitions of Khoisan life; a shell museum; the Da Gama Padrao – a stone cross donated by the Portuguese government; the Old Post Tree; and a Khoi (*Strandloper*) cave.

Wilderness

The natural beauty and tranquillity of the Wilderness area has made it a popular holiday destination since the late 1800s. Situated between the Kaaimans River and the Goukamma Nature Reserve some 15km east of George, the region is renowned for its endless stretches of beach and prolific bird life. Facilities include hiking, bird watching, mountain biking, horse riding, and hang-gliding and paragliding. Accommodation offered ranges from hotels, guesthouses, bed and breakfast and self-catering options, to caravan and camp sites.

Knysna

Knysna is one of the main tourist centres of the Garden Route offering dramatic scenery, a host of leisure activities and superb shopping. The town's main feature is the lagoon, a protected marine reserve that provides sanctuary for the endangered seahorse and the pansy shell. The entrance to the lagoon, guarded by two large sandstone cliffs, is known as The Heads. The name Knysna is thought to be a Khoikhoi word meaning 'straight down', which could refer to the sheerness of the cliffs at The Heads.

Activities offered include swimming, boating, fishing, canoeing, snorkelling and scuba diving, hiking and biking trails through the indigenous Knysna forest, and oyster tasting. The town itself is full of interesting art and craft boutiques, art galleries, indigenous wood furniture shops, restaurants, coffee shops, pubs, and places of historic and cultural interest. The Knysna Museum, the Angling Museum, the Knysna Oyster Beds, Millwood House, St. George's Church, and the Featherbed Nature Reserve on the western side of The Heads, are all places of interest worth visiting.

Plettenberg Bay

Plettenberg Bay is one of the country's top tourist hotspots during the summer season and has a host of hotels, restaurants, bars and shops. Situated among indigenous forests, the town has plenty of attractions for nature lovers. Places worth visiting include Nature's Valley, the Robberg Nature Reserve, the Keurbooms River Nature Reserve, Keurboomstrand and the Tsitsikamma National Park which is situated just to the east of the town. Historical sites within the area include the Old Whaling Station, St Andrew's Chapel, the Old Timber Shed and Forest Hall. The bay is home to a host of marine life including dolphins and whales and has a large variety of bird life.

The greater Plettenberg Bay area has large areas of unspoilt Cape flora, wetlands and lagoons, forests, sand dunes and long stretches of beach and is home to over 200 species of bird life. There are regular sightings of common and bottlenose dolphin, as well as Humpback, Brydes, Minke, Orca, and Southern Right whales. The region is also the largest breeding ground of the pansy shell (sand dollar).

West Coast

The West Coast is made up of a flat coastal belt, the Sandveld, and a fertile interior, known as the Swartland. Further to the north lies the Cederberg Wilderness area.

The region, although a popular destination for South African tourists, has been somewhat neglected by international tourists. However, the inviting natural beauty of the West Coast and the springtime showing of wildflowers in the Namaqualand area have successfully beckoned overseas visitors, so that greater interest has emerged in recent years.

The area has much to offer nature lovers, with numerous walks and hiking trails, an abundance of flora and fauna and rich variety of bird life. Its climate is mostly dry, hot and windy in summer. Winters can be very cold, especially late at night and early in the morning. The region is easily reached via the N7, which follows the coastline from Cape Town to Springbok in Northern Cape Province.

Tourism Destinations Southern Africa

Coastal Route

The West Coast National Park, isolated fishing villages, and scattered holiday resorts make up the Coastal Route. The area has a wealth of bird and marine life and a wide variety of sport and leisure pursuits. Fishing is a main source of income and there are many excellent seafood restaurants dotted along the coast. The weather is generally warmer and drier than Cape Town.

Langebaan

Located just over an hour's drive from Cape Town, the resort town is situated on the Langebaan Lagoon and has much to offer nature lovers and water sport enthusiasts alike.

Lambert's Bay

Lambert's Bay is a popular holiday town known for its open-air seafood and meat braai restaurants such as the Muisbosskerm and Bosduifklip. Countless flamingos are to be found on the Jakkalsvlei, and nearby Bird Island is an important breeding ground for Cape gannets and well as jackass penguins and the Cape cormorant. A boat charter runs hour-long cruises on the lookout for seals and dolphins. The Sandveld Museum, which depicts this region's history, is worth a visit.

Swartland

The interior region of the West Coast is an important wheat and wine growing area of South Africa, also known for its displays of wild flowers during the springtime. Temperatures in the region can become high during summer but are often cooled by the sea breezes of the Atlantic Ocean.

Clanwilliam

Clanwilliam is one of the ten oldest towns in South Africa and is a popular tourist venue, especially during the springtime wild flower season. Places of interest within the region include the Ramskop Nature Reserve and wildflower garden, Rooibos Tea Factory and the Clanwilliam Dam, a major venue for camping, picnicking and water sports.

Cederberg Wilderness Area

The Cederberg Wilderness Area was named after the large amount of cedar trees that once covered the higher slopes of the mountain. During the 18th century the forests were exploited for their timber and very few of these magnificent trees are to be found in the area today – restoration of the forest will take a few centuries. The area is a favourite venue for photographers and artists as well as for walking and hiking enthusiasts. Along the trails lie numerous streams, waterfalls and strangely shaped sandstone rock formations, as well as fine examples of rock art.

Overberg

The Overberg lies at the southern tip of Africa. Its major tourist attractions are Cape Agulhas, the town of Hermanus, the Shipwreck Museum in Bredasdorp, the Bontebok National Park and the De Hoop Nature Reserve. The region is known for its abundance of bird life, walking and hiking trails, whale watching, fishing, diving, 4 x 4 and mountain bike trails and canoeing.

Cape Agulhas

Cape Agulhas is the southernmost tip of Africa. One kilometre west of its lighthouse is the demarcation line of the true boundaries of the Atlantic and Indian Oceans. Places worth visiting are the Cape Agulhas Lighthouse and Lighthouse Museum as well as the Shipwreck Museum in nearby Bredasdorp.

Hermanus

The popular seaside resort of Hermanus is famous for whale watching and the Whale Crier who announces the sighting of whales by sounding his kelp horn. The resort has safe beaches and boasts some fine hiking trails and rock angling opportunities.

There are several wine estates in the area, most of which are open for tastings and sales.

▷ *A view of the Old Harbour at Hermanus*

Great Karoo

The N1 highway cuts a swath through the vast expanse of dry endless plains and empty horizons that is the terrain of the Great Karoo. The Karoo National Park, the well-preserved Victorian Village of Matjiesfontein and the picturesque town of Prince Albert are among the places of interest to visitors. The region is particularly popular with 4x4 trail drivers, mountain bikers and hikers.

Klein Karoo

The Klein Karoo is an area of semi-desert that produces excellent wines, raisins and other dried fruit. The region boasts two of South Africa's main tourist attractions – the ostrich show farms and the Cango Caves in the Oudtshoorn vicinity. Other tourist attractions within the region include the Gamka Mountain Reserve, home to the endangered Cape mountain zebra, and the Meiringspoort Gorge and Waterfall located in the Swartberg mountain range. The region also provides a host of sport and leisure opportunities such as 4x4 trails, mountain biking, horse riding and hiking.

Oudtshoorn

The town of Oudtshoorn is the heart of the ostrich-farming industry and a favourite destination for visitors to the Klein Karoo. The town became known as the Feather Capital of the World and prospered during the late-Victorian and Edwardian eras when ostrich feathers were high fashion. A reminder of the extravagance of this bygone age is found at the CP Nel Museum. There are three main ostrich show farms in the area – Highgate, Cango and Safari – all offering guided tours.

Cango Caves and Museum

The caves, situated some 30km from Oudtshoorn, consist of a series of spectacular limestone caverns filled with a variety of multicoloured, strangely shaped stalagmites and stalactites. Tours are conducted and there is a restaurant and curio shop, as well as a crèche for small children.

The Breede (Bree) River Valley

The Breede River Valley is a rich and fertile region of Western Cape. Spectacular passes in the awesome mountain ranges provide breathtaking views of deep verdant valleys – the setting of many picturesque towns. The area's scenic beauty is enhanced by its ever-changing vegetation that varies from springtime fruit blossoms to the kaleidoscopic hues of autumn leaves on the vine. Numerous mountain streams feed into the Breede River, which ensures the vineyards and fruit orchards in the valley are well watered. The region is one of the nation's main wine and fruit producers and is home to several of the country's top racehorse stud-farms.

Although the Breede River Valley is not one of the province's main tourist destinations, it is often the choice for a weekend getaway and can be reached in less than an hour from Cape Town via the Huguenot Toll Tunnel. It has much to offer by way of its beautifully restored buildings, interesting museums and historic sites, walking and hiking trails, as well as a wide choice of leisure and sport facilities. Specially laid out 4 x 4 trails, mountain biking, cycling, river canoeing, horse riding trails, fishing and rock climbing areas are included in the mix. The region has a wide variety of accommodation choices to suit all tastes and budgets.

Worcester

Worcester is the main centre of the Breede River Valley and is South Africa's largest wine-producing region. Places of interest include historic Church Street, the Karoo National Botanical Garden, the KWV Brandy Cellar, and the open-air living museum at Kleinplasie where the lifestyle of the early pioneers is re-enacted.

McGregor

McGregor is noted for its well-preserved buildings and fine examples of Victorian and Cape–Dutch architecture. The nearby Vrolijkheid Nature Reserve is a popular area for bird watching and hiking.

Ceres

Ceres is one of the most important deciduous fruit and fruit juice producing areas in South Africa. Situated among the mountains of the Skurweberg, Witsenberg and Hex River ranges, the area boasts several outstandingly beautiful scenic drives such as that over the Theronsberg Pass and Gydo Pass.

Other places of interest within the region include the cheese factory in the Bonnievale valley, Goudini Spa and the hot mineral springs at Montagu. There are popular tractor rides to the top of the Langeberg in the Mountagu district, and the Sadawa Game Reserve, which lies some 66km from Ceres, is worth a visit.

Activity

(a) List ten places of interest situated within Cape Town.

(b) Describe the attractions and activities available at the following popular tourist destinations in Western Cape:

Hout Bay, Cape Point, Stellenbosch, Franschhoek, Knysna, Plettenberg Bay and Oudtshoorn.

EASTERN CAPE

Facts at a Glance

Capital	Bisho
Size	169 580 sq km
Population	6,3m
Average Temperature	Summer min 16°C/max 25°C
– Port Elizabeth	Winter min 7°C/max 19°C
Main Languages	isiXhosa, English, Afrikaans

Geographical Outline

KwaZulu-Natal forms the north-eastern boundary of Eastern Cape Province; the Kingdom of Lesotho and Free State lie to the north; and to the north-west and west are Northern Cape and Western Cape provinces respectively. The waters of the Indian Ocean are the eastern boundary. The vegetation is immensely diverse ranging from lush indigenous forests along the coast, to savannah, grasslands and arid Karoo scrub in the interior.

It is home to several mountain ranges including the Kougaberge, Baviaanskloof-berge and the Grootwinterhoekberge, the Sneeuberge, Bamboesberg, Stormberge, Winterberge and Witteberge. Important rivers of the region include the Great Fish, Great Kei, Storms, Sundays and Gamtoos. The Gariep Dam, the largest in the country, is situated along its border with Free State.

Introduction

The Region

Eastern Cape is a popular holiday destination among South Africans. Its attractions are in endless white-sand beaches, a rich diversity of sporting activities and game and nature reserves.

The region was frontier territory until the latter part of the 19th century and saw many historic battles fought for the possession of land. Museums and historic sites bear testimony to a turbulent past.

The Economy

Port Elizabeth and Uitenhage are the centres of the South African motor industry. The province has fairly substantial farming interests concerned with citrus fruit, sheep (lamb/mutton and wool), cattle (beef and dairy products), angora goats/mohair.

The Importance of Tourism

The province is fairly underdeveloped from a tourism point of view, but it has great potential as a holiday destination.

Climate

Eastern Cape's climate is diverse and because its coastal regions lie between the subtropical zone of KwaZulu-Natal and the Mediterranean conditions of Western Cape, the climate along the coast tends to be influenced by its nearness to either of these regions. Conditions in the interior vary from the dry or semi-arid regions of the Karoo, which experience long hot summers and moderate winters, to the towns close to the Free State border where the rise in altitude lowers the temperature.

Transportation and Accessibility

Road

Several national routes traverse the province connecting its main centres with those of the rest of the country. The N6 runs down from Bloemfontein in Free State, through Eastern Cape towns of Aliwal North, Queenstown and Stutterheim to East London, where it joins the main N2 artery that follows the coastline to the north and south. The N10 from Northern Cape enters the province at Middelburg, passing through Cradock and Cookhouse and on to the coast, connecting with the N2 between Grahamstown and Port Elizabeth. The N9, at the Middleburg interchange, goes through Graaff Reinet, Aberdeen and Willowmore and continues into the eastern part of Western Cape Province. Within the Wild Coast region, many of the roads are in poor condition. Caution is advised, particularly when driving at night, because the incidence of potholes and roaming cattle puts motorists at risk of having an accident and being stranded in an isolated area.

Regular coach services operate from Port Elizabeth and East London to most major centres including Johannesburg, Pretoria, Cape Town and Durban. Numerous car hire companies operate throughout Eastern Cape and offices are located at the airport and in most town centres.

Air

There are regular flights from East London and Port Elizabeth to the major airports in the country, and between Umtata and Johannesburg.

Rail

The province has an extensive rail network with mainline trains operating from East London and Port Elizabeth to Johannesburg. The 'Apple Express' narrow-gauge steam train operates between Port Elizabeth and Thornhill.

Accommodation

Accommodation is plentiful within the region's main tourist areas. Most large towns and coastal resorts have a choice ranging from hotels, guesthouses, bed and breakfast and self-catering units, to camp and caravan facilities. A number of game reserves offer self-contained lodgings, camp and caravan sites.

Sun International has four upmarket resort complexes located within Eastern Cape – Wild Coast Sun and Casino, Fish River Sun and Casino, the Mpekwene Sun and the Amatola Sun.

Wild Coast Sun and Casino

The Wild Coast Sun is located along Eastern Cape's enchanting coastline, not far from its border with KwaZulu-Natal. It is a luxury hotel and casino complex which offers its guests a full range of recreational facilities.

The Fish River Sun

Situated along the southern part of the coastline close to Port Alfred, the Fish River Sun Hotel and Casino resort has an 18-hole golf course in a wonderful setting, as well as a swimming pool, and tennis and squash courts. The complex can accommodate up to 200 delegates in its conference facilities.

The Mpekwene Sun Marine Resort

The Mpekwene Sun Marine Resort is a luxury hotel located a short distance from the Fish River Sun. The complex offers a variety of entertainment and pursuits such as hiking, tennis and squash, as well as water sport activities.

The Amatola Sun

Located at the foot of the Amatola Mountains near Bisho, the hotel offers a wide choice of sport activities, including a 9-hole mashie golf course, tennis, swimming, volleyball, squash and bowls. There is also a small casino.

Historic Highlights

Eastern Cape Province was first settled by the Stone Age San and later the pastoral Khoikhoi.

It is believed that Cape Nguni or Xhosa-speaking people were already living in the region around the Umthatha River as early as 1593.

Bartolomeu Dias sailed along the eastern coast as far as Algoa Bay during his voyages of discovery in 1488.

As the Dutch of the Cape continued to expand their frontiers eastwards, conflict arose between the Xhosa and Boer farmers, which resulted in several frontier wars.

Grahamstown, founded by John Graham in 1812, grew into a main commercial and trading centre.

In 1820 British Settlers were brought to the region in an attempt to control the conflict between Xhosa and *trekboers* (migratory Dutch farmers).

In 1857 a young Xhosa girl named Nongqawuse had a vision which had a significant impact on the lives of the Xhosa people. She claimed that the ancestors would drive the white people into the sea from which they came if her people sacrificed all their cattle and crops. The people did as she said and the consequences became known as 'the national suicide of the Xhosa' – no ancestors appeared on the specified day, neither was there a return of cattle and crops – more than 25 000 Xhosa died of starvation and many more were forced to migrate.

Population

The population of Eastern Cape consists mainly of Xhosa people and those of European descent, including Dutch, British and German.

Social and Cultural Profile

The people who settled in Eastern Cape over the centuries have made an indelible mark on its cultural heritage. It is believed that the Xhosa people were living in the Umtata region as early as 1593. Their traditional lifestyle and distinct culture is very much in evidence in the region. For the benefit of visitors, fascinating arts and crafts are displayed and traditional songs and dances performed in many cultural centres.

People of European descent have made a strong impact on the social, cultural and economic history of the area, developing a thriving wool industry, as well as an art and education centre.

Eastern Cape is home to some of the country's most outstanding architecture, ranging from the traditional Karoo homesteads to fine examples of Victorian and Georgian style buildings.

▷ *A Xhosa woman*

Sport and Leisure Facilities

Eastern Cape boasts a wide variety of facilities for sport and recreation. There are numerous hiking trails in the region and the entire coastline is a haven for anglers, surfers, scuba divers and water sport enthusiasts. Information on the best sites and venues is available from the various tourist information offices. Most towns in the province offer facilities for all the major sports such as golf, bowling, tennis, squash, rugby, cricket and soccer.

Hiking

The region is known for its many and varied hiking trails. Information on trails is available at tourist information offices. The 25-day Wild Coast Hiking Trail follows the entire coastline from the Mtamvuna estuary near Port Edward to the Great Kei

River Mouth. The trail may be split into five shorter sections. Other popular trails include the 41km, 5-day Otter Trail between the Storms River Mouth in the Tsitsikamma National Park and Nature's Valley; the 64 km, 5-day Tsitsikamma Hiking Trail, which runs through the foothills of the Tsitsikamma Mountains; the 105km, 6-day Amatola Hiking Trail through the Amatola Mountains; the 31km, 3-day Mountain Zebra Hiking Trail through the Fonteinkloof and Grootkloof Gorges and on to the Bankberg; and the 32km, 2-day Hogsback Hiking Trail.

Fishing

In addition to deep-sea game fishing, Eastern Cape offers opportunities for fly, surf, rock and gully fishing and boasts some of the country's finest angling spots.

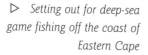 ▷ *Setting out for deep-sea game fishing off the coast of Eastern Cape*

Mountain Biking

Many mountain biking trails have been established throughout the province and include those in the rugged terrain of the Longmore Forest and in the beautiful areas of the Baakens River and the Van Staden's Wildflower Reserve.

Diving

Eastern Cape's coastline provides numerous diving sites, some of which include wreck dives. Information on sites is provided at the East London Museum and at various diving centres along the coast where courses, equipment and charters are also available. A snorkelling and scuba diving trail exists in the Tsitsikamma National Park, which includes reef and tidal pool snorkelling.

Canoeing

The Fish River is considered to be one of the world's best white water rivers and is the site of the Sunseeker and Fish River Canoe Marathon. Excursions are held on the river most days, through the Cradock canoeing club.

Snow-Skiing

Snow-skiing facilities, which include instruction and the hiring of ski equipment, exist at the Tiffindell resort situated some 25km from the village of Rhodes.

Cricket

Port Elizabeth is home to St. George's Park, one of South Africa's premier cricket grounds where both national and international matches are played throughout the summer season.

Conservation and Eco-Tourism

Several parks and reserves have been established in the region to preserve indigenous plants, animals and bird life. The successful work carried out at Addo Elephant Park and Mountain Zebra National Park is a demonstration of the concern with mammals that were close to extinction in the area. The Lammergier Private Nature Reserve provides a sanctuary for endangered birds including the bearded vulture (lammergier) and Cape vulture, and the Karringmelk Cape Vulture Sanctuary is a breeding ground for these birds. Parks such as the Van Staden's Wildflower Reserve and the Tsitsikamma National Park protect the region's indigenous flora, and the 355ha Cape Recife Nature Reserve, situated close to Port Elizabeth, protects the beach and natural dune vegetation, as well as the many birds of the area, including penguins.

Wildlife Parks and Nature Reserves

Eastern Cape's wildlife parks and reserves offer visitors a chance to view Africa's game without having to venture further north where precautions against malaria are necessary.

Addo Elephant Park

Situated some 72km from Port Elizabeth, the Addo Elephant Park is set among indigenous bush country around the Sundays River Valley and is one of the region's main tourist attractions. Established in 1931 to protect the elephant population of the south-east Cape, the park is now home to about 300 elephants. Sanctuary is also provided for the East African black rhinoceros, as well as buffalo, caracal (lynx), aardvark, jackal, antelope (several species) and over 170 different types of bird. The park has some 43km of gravel roads, a 6km 4-hour hiking trail through a fenced-off area, two hides, a restaurant, curio shop, and braai (barbecue) and picnic facilities. Night drives can be booked through the camp office. Accommodation is available in cottages, chalets or huts and there is a caravan and camp site.

Mountain Zebra National Park

The Mountain Zebra National Park, established in 1937 to protect the mountain zebra from extinction, is located some 25km west of Cradock. The park now boasts a herd of over 200 zebra, various species of antelope, caracal, baboon, jackal and the bat-eared fox and is also home to some 200 species of bird, including Cape eagle owls. Game viewing options include travelling by car along the reserve's 37km of road, by foot or on horseback. Accommodation is available in chalets or at the camp and caravan site.

Shamwari Game Reserve

The 14 000ha Shamwari Game Reserve lies some 72km to the east of Port Elizabeth along the Bushmans River. The reserve has reintroduced many of the mammals hunted out of the region, including lion, rhino, elephant, buffalo, leopard and hippo, as well as a large variety of antelope and bird life. Game drives accompanied by rangers, walking safaris and night drives are available. Accommodation is available in thatched chalets or refurbished settler houses.

Tsitsikamma National Park

The Tsitsikamma National Park is Africa's first marine park. Situated 615km from Cape Town and 195km from Port Elizabeth, it lies in a region where the forest meets the sea. The boundaries of the park reach almost 80km along the Cape coastline and extend some 5km into the ocean. Its forest is rich in indigenous flora and home to a wide variety of bird life, as well as bushbuck, grysbok, duikers, baboon, the vervet monkey and Cape clawless otter. Recreational activities include scuba diving, snorkelling, angling, bathing and several nature trails. The park has two rest camps, providing accommodation in cottages or huts, as well as camping and caravan facilities.

Van Staden's Wildflower Reserve

Situated close to the Van Staden's River Mouth, this 500ha reserve is divided in two by the N2 highway. The southern forest is home to many of the region's indigenous trees, whereas the northern plateau is covered with fynbos. There are two short trails through the park – the 3km River Walk and the 2km Forest Walk – as well as several picnic sites.

Tourist Attractions

Western Region

Port Elizabeth

Port Elizabeth is known as The Friendly City and is one of the gateways to the Eastern Cape region. It is the largest coastal city between Durban and Cape Town and is easily reached by land and air.

The region has numerous beaches and an abundance of water sport activities. The city itself is steeped in history. Places worth visiting include the Donkin Heritage Trail – a 5km walk which takes in the most important monuments, buildings, churches and gardens around the centre of the city – and the Port Elizabeth Museum. There are several walks and hiking trails of varying lengths in and around the area, a number of wildlife and nature reserves and numerous braai and picnic spots. The Apple Express, a narrow-gauge steam train, operates between Port Elizabeth and Thornhill. Facilities for sport include golf, bowls, cricket and rugby.

Jeffrey's Bay

One of the most popular coastal areas in Eastern Cape, Jeffrey's Bay is known among surfers as the 'home of the perfect wave' and is host to the annual Billabong Country Feeling Surf Classic competition held in July. The area is known for its beautiful beaches, diving, fishing and bird watching.

Grahamstown

Grahamstown was established in 1812 around a fort built after the Fourth Frontier War. The town grew when the 1820 Settlers, disillusioned with farming, took up residence and began practising the skills they had learnt in England. Grahamstown boasts several impressive buildings and places of interest including the 1820 Wildflower Reserve, the Old Provost, Albany Museum, Observatory Museum, the 1820 Settlers National Monument, and the JLB Smith Institute of Ichthyology, where the second coelacanth caught off the Comoro Islands is exhibited.

A variety of accommodation options exist within the town including several historic hotels, such as the Cathcart Arms and The Grand.

Port Alfred

Port Alfred is one of the province's prime holiday destinations and a rallying point for water sport enthusiasts, including surfers and divers. Other popular sports catered for in the area are angling, deep-sea game fishing, canoeing, golf and hiking.

Kenton on Sea

Situated between the estuaries of the Bushmans and Kariega rivers, Kenton on Sea is a very well-patronised seaside holiday destination, particularly for family vacations. The resort has a variety of activities including golf, tennis, bowls, squash, angling, and canoeing up the Bushmans River. Places of interest include the replica of the stone cross erected by Bartolomeu Dias, situated 6m from the town centre, and the Joan Muirhead Nature Reserve which protects the land between the two rivers.

The Karoo

The Karoo is a semi-desert region of vast open spaces and distant mountain ranges, where sheep, angora goats, cattle and horse farming provide the backbone of the economy. The region boasts several nature reserves, including the Karoo Nature Reserve and Mountain Zebra National Park, established to protect the unique flora and fauna of the region; many picturesque towns rich in history and fine architecture; and a variety of sport and leisure opportunities.

The Karoo town of Cradock was the home of one of South Africa's well-known authors, Olive Schreiner, who wrote the famous work, *Story of an African Farm*, in 1883. The author's former house is now a museum that displays facets of her life, and the town's library has a fine collection of her works. Her grave is situated at the top of Buffelskop Mountain and can be reached by way of a three-hour hike.

Graaff Reinet

Known as the 'Gem of the Karoo', the historic town of Graaff Reinet is being restored to its former glory. Founded in 1786, it is one of the oldest towns in Eastern Cape and has many museums and art galleries, 200 national monuments and examples of fine architecture ranging from Cape–Dutch to Victorian and typical Karoo-style cottages. The town is situated at the foothills of the Sneeuberg Mountains and is surrounded by the Karoo Nature Reserve, which has numerous species of antelope and more than 200 species of bird. There are hiking trails, as well as water sport and angling possibilities at the Van Ryneveld Pass Dam. The Valley of Desolation, located just outside of the town, is considered to be one of South Africa's scenic wonders. It has weird dolerite pillars formed over millions of years of erosion whereby the surrounding sedimentary rock has weathered more quickly than the dolerite which can stand as tall as 120 metres.

Nieu-Bethesda

Nieu-Bethesda lies some 50km north-west of Graaff Reinet and is a tourist detour made famous by Helen Martins who transformed her home and garden with a collection of unusual figures. Known as the Owl House, it was opened as a museum in 1992. The venue is the setting of Athol Fugard's play, *The Road to Mecca*.

Amatola Region

East London

East London is a river port situated at the mouth of the Buffalo River. It is a popular family-orientated holiday destination with white-sand beaches and beautiful parks and gardens. Among the many places of interest in and around the town are the Aquarium and the East London Museum. Famous for its specimen of the coelacanth fish and the world's only dodo egg, the museum also exhibits fine examples of the nation's traditional cultures. The Umtiza Forest, home to ancient cycads and umtiza trees, the Gonubie Sanctuary, Mpongo Park, and the Dierama Reserve are other tourist attractions, as are the City Hall, the German Settler Memorial, and Lock Street Gaol shopping area.

▷ *German Settlers Memorial in East London*

Hogsback

Hogsback is one of South Africa's popular eco-tourism destinations boasting an ecology shrine dedicated to the preservation of the town's fragile ecosystem. The region encompasses the Hogsback State Forest, the Auckland Nature Reserve and the forests of the Tyume River Valley. The area has numerous trails varying from short 3km rambles to two-day hikes. Information on the various trails and places of historic interest in the vicinity is available in the local booklet, *Exploring Hogsback*. There are several hotels, guesthouses and bed and breakfast establishments within the area, as well as a camp and caravan site.

Stutterheim

The town of Stutterheim is a popular eco-tourism and adventure sport destination. Places of interest include the grave of Chief Sandile and the Mgwali Xhosa Traditional Village. There are many hiking and nature trails in the area as well as the Double Drift Game Reserve, and Gubu and Wriggleswade dams.

Wild Coast Region

The Wild Coast

The Wild Coast's 280-km coastline is strewn with endless white-sand beaches washed by the warm waters of the Indian Ocean. The coast is treacherous to ships and as recently as 1991, the vessel *Oceanos* foundered, but all on board were rescued. Several 16th century wrecks, including passengers and cargo, lie beneath the turbulent waters. In 1999 a wreck was discovered and is thought to be that of the *Waratah*.

The hinterland consists of rugged terrain filled with magnificent indigenous forests, deep river gorges and a profusion of flora and fauna. There are a number of small nature reserves throughout the region and the area is a favourite with hikers, anglers and divers. Accommodation ranges from luxury resorts to numerous small hotels and guesthouses, and camp and caravan sites.

Coffee Bay

Situated at the mouth of the Nenga River, Coffee Bay is a seaside resort that offers good surf, swimming, fishing, walking, riding and golf. Popular accommodation in the area includes the Ocean View Hotel, the Anchorage Hotel and caravan and camping facilities.

Hole-in-the-Wall

A large detached cliff, lying offshore about 8km along the beach south of Coffee Bay, has a huge tunnel caused through natural erosion by the sea. This natural formation was named Hole-in-the-Wall by an English ship's captain in 1823.

The resort at the site offers lunches at the hotel of the same name, and self-catering accommodation at Holiday Village. There are several short walks up the coastline or through the surrounding dense coastal forest and hills as well as angling opportunities.

Port St Johns

Port St Johns is situated at the Mzimvubu River mouth. It is surrounded by beautiful forests and fine beaches and has countless opportunities for walking, swimming and fishing.

Mazeppa Bay

Deep-water angling on the adjoining island as well as kite fishing at Shark Point and Boiling Pot are popular pastimes in the Mazeppa Bay area. The resort has three palm-fringed beaches and an excellent hotel. It is a favourite spot for swimming, picnicking and shell collecting.

Historic Sites

There are numerous places of historic interest scattered throughout the province. San rock art sites and several monuments and battle sites are found in towns such as Lady Grey and Aliwal North.

Examples of rock art are also found in Dordrecht, Jamestown and the Maclear and Ugie district, and there is a 32m long art gallery on the farm Denorbin, situated just above Barkly Pass on the road to Elliot. Towns such as Adelaide, Fort Beaufort, Peddie and Whittlesea in the Amatola district started out as forts or military outposts during the period of the Frontier Wars and still maintain several historic sites, fine museums and architecture.

Cultural Villages

Cultural villages and centres exist throughout the province, allowing visitors to enjoy an authentic cultural experience that includes traditional song and dance as well as an appreciation of local handicrafts. Popular venues include Kaya Lendaba, situated in the Shamwari Private Game Reserve, which is South Africa's only African Traditional Healing Village. The centre is involved with the preservation of ancient rituals, sacred practices and customs. Exposure to other cultures is offered at the Masithandane Association in Grahamstown and on Umthati Township Tours. In addition, the Mgwali Xhosa Traditional Village near Stutterheim gives visitors a chance to experience Xhosa culture, and the Isinamva Cultural Village situated close to Mount Frere gives an insight into the culture of the Bhaca Xhosa.

Activity

Identify five different types of sport activity well catered for in Eastern Cape.

KINGDOM OF LESOTHO

Facts at a Glance

Capital	Maseru
Size	30 355 sq km
Population	2,1m
Currency	1 loti (plural: maloti) = 100 lisente
Average Temperature – Maseru	Summer min 14°C/max 24°C
	Winter min –5°C/max 16°C
Main Languages	seSotho, English
Main Religions	Christianity, Indigenous Beliefs
Time Zone	GMT+2

Geographical Outline

The landlocked country of Lesotho is completely surrounded by South Africa. The breathtakingly beautiful Maluti and Drakensberg mountains dominate the country, with Mount Thabana Ntlenyana the highest peak, standing at 3 482m. Numerous rivers traverse the country, including the Senqu (Orange River) and Caledon. The important Katse Dam is part of the Highlands Water Project.

Introduction

The Region

The Kingdom of Lesotho has spectacular mountain scenery and offers a host of related outdoor activities. Its seasons are more pronounced than in neighbouring South Africa. Springtime sees the nation's villages festooned with peach blossom and the mountain plateaus covered with alpine flowers; summer is a time for river rafting and canoeing; autumn for hiking and pony-trekking; and winter for snow skiing in the mountains.

The Economy

Lesotho's economy is based mainly on agriculture, light manufacturing and remittances from miners who are employed in South Africa. Subsistence farming supports the households of the majority of rural people.

The nation's major natural resource is water and the recently developed Highlands Water Project provides water and hydroelectricity to the nation and parts of South Africa.

The Importance of Tourism

Although Lesotho's tourism industry is fairly small and underdeveloped, many tourists come to enjoy the unique mountain scenery and traditional lifestyles found within the country's borders. It is popular with four-wheel-drive enthusiasts and nature lovers, who hike, climb and pony-trek through the remote regions of the country.

Tourism was dealt a serious blow due to recent unrest, and many of its buildings were burnt down or damaged. At one stage, in 1998, the situation led to South African National Defence Force troops entering the country.

It is prohibited to take photographs of certain buildings within the country, such as the Palace, airports and government buildings. It is advisable to ask prior to taking a photograph if you are unsure.

Climate

Lesotho's mountainous terrain plays a major role in the country's climatic diversity with temperatures varying dramatically according to altitude. Summer temperatures can be fairly hot, especially in the lowlands, and winters bitterly cold, with snow on the highlands. Rain falls mainly between October and April and late afternoon storms are not unusual. It should be noted that as Lesotho is a mountainous region prone to sudden changes in weather, rainwear and warm clothing are always recommended for the traveller.

Transportation and Accessibility

Road

Within the country the Main North Road and Main South Road provide access to most centres. However, many of the roads in the southern and eastern part of Lesotho require four-wheel-drive vehicles.

Car hire facilities are available through agents in Maseru.

Border Crossings

Lesotho can be entered by road via numerous border posts from South Africa. The main posts are Ficksburgbrug and Maserubrug (24 hours) and the Sani Pass (08:00–16:00).

Rail

No passenger trains operate within Lesotho.

Air

SA Airlink and Air Lesotho operate between Moshoeshoe I International Airport, in Maseru, and Johannesburg. International and regional links are mainly via Johannesburg. Various private air charter companies in South Africa operate into Lesotho. There is an M20 Airport Departure Tax.

Visa Requirements

Most citizens, including South Africans, British and Americans, do not require a visa to enter Lesotho.

Accommodation

Lesotho has several good hotels and lodges offering a variety of accommodation – from the luxury Lesotho Sun in Maseru to rustic self-catering lodges set amid the captivating mountain scenery. Many of the hotels and lodges organise hikes and pony-treks into the surrounding area. It is also possible to organise a stay with a Basotho family for a firsthand experience of their way of life. Information on accommodation is available from the tourist information centre.

Although there are very few caravan and camp sites within Lesotho, visitors are allowed to camp in the rural areas as long as permission is obtained from the local Headman or Chief.

Health

Good medical facilities are available in the main centres of Lesotho. The Flying Doctor service provides emergency medical care to the remote regions of the country. Malaria is not common within Lesotho and its rivers are bilharzia free.

Historic Highlights

Between 1815 and 1829 King Moshoeshoe the Great (also called Moshesh) forged a powerful nation from the twenty-three clans scattered by the *Difaqane* Wars and established strongholds at Butha-Buthe and Thaba Bosiu (the Mountain of Night).

The arrival of the Boers into the region after 1830 saw Moshesh ally himself with the British and the country become a British colony known as Basutoland.

On 4 October 1966 the Kingdom of Lesotho became a fully independent nation.

Today's ruling monarch, King Letsie III, is a great-grandson of King Moshoeshoe I.

Population

The majority of the population are Basotho and there are small minorities of people of European and Chinese descent who live within the borders of Lesotho.

Social and Cultural Profile

The nation is steeped in culture and has retained many of its traditions, with music, dance and age-old ceremonies still very much a way of life. The family unit and village is of great importance and respect is shown to the elder generation. The traditional Basotho stone hut may be seen throughout the land and oxen are still used for the ploughing and harvesting of crops in many areas.

The Basotho pony was for a long time the only means of transport through most of the country's terrain and it is not uncommon to see a Basotho horseman riding by dressed in his brightly coloured blanket and distinctive conical straw hat.

The skill of crafting has been handed down through generations. The products are mostly items for everyday use, such as the traditional Basotho hat, clay pots and jugs, mats and baskets, as well as jewellery and finely woven wool and mohair. Most items have now become popular export items and there are several craft centres where wall-hangings, tapestries and rugs are created by hand from wool spun on the premises.

Religion

The majority of the people of Lesotho are Christians belonging to the Roman Catholic, Anglican and Evangelical churches. Around 20 per cent of the population follow indigenous beliefs and there is a small minority of Muslims. Many of the Christian adherents incorporate indigenous beliefs into their religious practices.

Cuisine

Traditional food consists of beef, chicken and pork served with mealie meal, potatoes or rice, vegetables and fruit.

Festivals and Events

Important dates in the Lesotho calendar include New Year's Day, Moshoeshoe's Day on 11 March, Heroes' Day on 4 April, Easter, Workers' Day on 1 May, Ascension Day, the King's Birthday on 17 July, National Independence Day on 4 October, Christmas Day and Boxing Day on 25th and 26th December.

Sport and Leisure Facilities

Lesotho's outdoor activities are one of its major drawcards and facilities exist for a host of activities, varying from adventure sport to leisurely games of tennis. Newly introduced sports gaining in popularity throughout the region include canoeing, river rafting and mountain biking.

Walking and Hiking

An abundance of walking and hiking trails criss-cross the Lesotho countryside. Trails can be taken from most mountain lodges and information is available at the tourist information centres and from local guides. Lesotho has several unique species of bird life and flora, which enhance the hiking experience.

Basotho Pony-Trekking

There are numerous pony-trekking centres located throughout the country, offering journeys varying from one hour to several days. This unique experience offers visitors a chance to view the superb scenery astride Basotho ponies, accompanied by experienced guides, and to imbibe the local way of life during stopovers at traditional villages.

Fishing

The country has much to offer the angling enthusiast. Popular spots include the confluence of the Ts'ehlanyane and Tlholohatsi rivers at Butha-Buthe, the Khubelu and Mokhotlong rivers near Mokhotlong, the Tsoelikane River at Qacha's Nek and at the Thaba-Tseka Dam. Details of the many different sites are available at the tourist information offices.

Mountain Climbing

Several organisations exist for visitors who wish to take advantage of the country's challenging mountain climbing opportunities. Information is available at the tourist information offices or through specialised companies.

Skiing

Skiing is a popular winter sport and ski boots and equipment can be hired at the Sani Top Chalet at the top of the Sani Pass.

4 x 4 Trails

Lesotho forms part of the popular Roof of Africa Scenic 4 x 4 Route in conjunction with KwaZulu-Natal and Free State in South Africa. This exciting route takes enthusiasts through the Maluti and Drakensberg mountain ranges. There are also several other trails found within the Kingdom. Information can be obtained from the Lesotho Tourist Board in Maseru.

Wildlife Parks and Nature Reserves

Sehlabathebe National Park

The Sehlabathebe National Park covers an area of some 6 500ha high on the Drakensberg escarpment. The park is popular for bird watching and the viewing of its alpine flora. Accommodation is available at the park's lodge and opportunities exist within the park for hiking, rock climbing, horse riding and fishing.

Tourist Attractions

Maseru

Maseru, Lesotho's capital, was founded in 1869. It has several fine hotels and restaurants, as well as a variety of nightlife venues, including two casinos. The recent civil unrest has seen many of the city's buildings and landmarks disappear.

Lesotho Highlands

The Highlands region is one of Lesotho's main tourist destinations, known for its spectacular scenery and traditional Basotho villages.

Katse Dam and Dam Wall

The Katse Dam is the centrepiece of the Highlands Water project. The scenery in this region is magnificent and plans are underway to make the Katse Lake area an important boating and recreation area.

Maletsunyane/Le Bihan Falls

The Maletsunyane or Le Bihan Falls are the highest in southern Africa, plunging some 192 metres. The region is a popular spot for hiking and horse-trekking. The rare spiral aloe, which is endemic to the region, is found on the mountains to the west of the falls.

Morija

Nestled at the foot of the Makhoarane Mountain is Morija, established in 1833 by French Protestant missionaries invited by Moshoeshoe to teach his people. Places of interest include the Morija Museum and Archives, which give an insight into the culture and history of the Basotho nation, and the nearby San paintings and dinosaur footprints.

Historic Sites

Dinosaur Fossils and Footprints

Evidence of Lesotho's prehistoric past can be seen in the many fossil remains and footprints of dinosaur found throughout the country. Examples can be found close to Subeng Stream, Leribe (Hlotse) at the Tsikoane Village, Morija, Moyeni and Masitise.

San Rock Art Sites

Many thousands of rock paintings found throughout the country testify to the fact that the San once inhabited the region. The best known rock art site is the magnificent gallery of paintings at Ha Baroana, also known as Ha Khotso, situated some 39 km east of Maseru.

Activity

Circle the type of client you would recommend to visit Lesotho:

young

enjoys relaxation

enjoys culture

sophisticated

adventurous

outdoor type

loves art galleries

enjoys nightlife

active

12 KINGDOM OF SWAZILAND

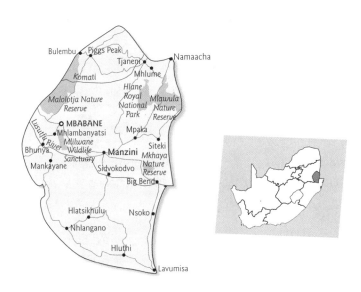

Facts at a Glance

Capital	Mbabane
Size	17 400 sq km
Population	1m
Currency	1 lilangeni = 100 cents
Average Temperature	Summer min 19°C/max 30°C
– Mbabane	Winter min 6°C/max 24°C
Main Languages	siSwati, English
Main Religions	Christianity, Indigenous Beliefs
Time	GMT+2

Geographical Outline

The Kingdom of Swaziland is landlocked by its borders with South Africa to the north, south and west, and the Lebombo Mountains that form much of its eastern border with Mozambique. The country's main rivers are the Komati, Mbuluzi and Lusutfu.

Its terrain varies from scenic mountains to lowveld savannah and covers a wide variety of different habitats demarcated as Highveld, Middleveld and Lowveld, and the Lebombo region.

Highveld

Situated in the north-west of the country is the Highveld region of mountains, forests and streams. This cool area is a popular tourism destination, especially the road through the Ezulwini Valley from Mbabane to Manzini.

Middleveld

This fertile and mainly agricultural area runs through the middle of the country and produces much of the country's crops, fruit and vegetables.

Lowveld

The Lowveld is a dry, hot, subtropical region characterised by typical African bush vegetation. Popular tourism destinations in this region include the Hlane Royal National Park.

Lebombo

The Lebombo region connects Swaziland with Maputaland to the south and Mpumalanga in the north. The area is home to the Mbuluzi Gorge and Mlawula Nature Reserve and is a popular venue for hikers and bird lovers.

Introduction

The Region

Swaziland has much to offer as a tourist destination. The beautiful diverse landscape, a land full of tradition and culture, a host of sport and leisure activities and an extensive choice of accommodation create an appealing mix that attracts the traveller.

The Economy

Important sectors of the economy include manufacturing (agro-processing) and agriculture with much of the population occupied in subsistence farming; those who are employed on South African mines remit a portion of their wages, which in effect boosts the economy. Important crops include sugar-cane, pineapples, cotton and tobacco. Most of the nation's imports come from South Africa.

The Importance of Tourism

Swaziland has several fine resorts offering a host of facilities and activities for visitors. Sun International has complexes situated throughout the country offering conference facilities as well as sport and leisure activities that include casinos, health spas, golf, tennis and bowling.
The Kingdom boasts several game and nature reserves providing a host of activities in diverse habitats.

Climate

Swaziland's climate varies according to region and altitude. Rain falls mainly during the summer months from November to March and afternoon thunderstorms are a regular occurrence. Summer temperatures can reach 40°C in the Lowveld regions, but are cooler in the Highveld. Winter days are warm in the Lowveld but can become cold, especially at night, in the Highveld.

Transportation and Accessibility

Road

All the main roads leading into Swaziland are tarred and the secondary gravel roads are well maintained. Caution is advised as many of the mountain roads are often steep and winding and speed limits should be strictly observed.

There is an efficient bus service that departs from Mbabane to all main centres within Swaziland, as well as a service to Johannesburg. Car hire facilities are available through well-known companies, with offices at Matsapha International Airport.

Border Crossings

There are twelve border crossings between Swaziland and South Africa. The busiest entrance points are at Golela (07:00–22:00), Oshoek (07:00–22:00) and Mahamba (07:00–22:00).

Rail

Swaziland's rail network is fairly small, linking the country to Maputo in Mozambique, and Richard's Bay and Durban in South Africa.

Air

Swaziland's Matsapha Airport is located 8km from Manzini. SA Airlink operates daily between Johannesburg and Manzini. Scan Air Charters fly small aircraft within the Kingdom. An E20 departure tax is payable when departing Swaziland by air.

Visa Requirements

All visitors to Swaziland require a valid passport or travel document. Most nationalities, including South Africans, British and American citizens, do not require a visa to enter the country.

Accommodation

There is no official grading system for accommodation within Swaziland. Facilities vary from top-priced luxury hotels to those with moderate tariffs, resorts, chalets, caravan and camp sites. Most of the country's game parks and nature reserves offer accommodation options.

Sun International hotels and resorts include the luxury Royal Swazi Sun Hotel and Country Club, the Nhlangano Sun Hotel and Casino, the Lugogo Sun, and the Ezulwini.

▷ *The swimming pool area at the Royal Swazi Sun Hotel*

Health

Malaria is endemic in certain parts of Swaziland and precautions should be taken.

Historic Highlights

Around 1750, Ngwane III settled in the region now known as Swaziland.

The Swazi nation became powerful during the *Mfecane* under King Sobhuza I who expanded the kingdom further, colonising Sotho, Tsonga and Nguni chiefdoms.

Europeans arrived in the area around 1836. When gold was discovered at Piggs Peak, large numbers of foreigners moved into the area and several land concessions were granted.

The region was administered by the Transvaal between 1894–1903 and by the British after the Anglo–Boer War.

One of the country's major setbacks was that most of the land was held by foreigners in the form of concessions. When Sobhuza II became king in 1921 he spent his resources on regaining the land for the Swazi nation.

Swaziland gained its independence from the United Kingdom on 6 September 1968.

Population

The majority of Swaziland's population is Swazi, with small minorities of Zulu, Shangaan and people of European descent.

▷ *A Swazi man in traditional dress*

Social and Cultural Profile

The Kingdom of Swaziland is a monarchy and an independent member of the Commonwealth. It is ruled by

His Majesty King Mswati III, the *Ngwenyama* of Swaziland, assisted by the Prime Minister, the Senate and the House of Assembly.

The country has a rich cultural heritage and many of its people still embrace age-old customs and traditions.

Choosing a King

The successor to the throne is chosen in relation to the status of his mother. The Royal Council plays an important role in the selection of the successor to the throne, and after the King's death, the Council chooses the Queen Mother from an unrelated family. If the successor is still a minor, the Queen Mother to the late King assumes responsibility of Regent until the prince is crowned. The present Queen Mother, Queen Ntombi, ruled as Queen Regent until King Mswati III was crowned in April 1986.

The Royal Dlamini line never intermarries; the Queen Mother is never a Dlamini. She may only have one son, as blood brothers may not succeed a king. The King and Queen Mother assist and advise each other.

Festivals and Events

Two of the most important cultural events that take place within the kingdom are the *Ncwala* and *Umhlanga* ceremonies. Photographs of these events may be taken only with prior permission, and certain parts of the Ncwala ceremony may neither be watched nor photographed.

The Ncwala Ceremony

The Ncwala or first fruit ceremony is certainly the most sacred of all the Swazi rituals. The King plays a dominant role and there is no ceremony when there is no reigning King. The date for the event is chosen by Swazi astrologers and is usually sometime in December or January.

The ceremony has various stages. The festivities begin with a journey by the Bemanti people to the rivers and ocean to collect certain herbs and water. On their return to the Royal Cattle Kraal the 'Little Ncwala' ceremony begins, preceding the appearance of the full moon. This is followed by the 'Big Ncwala' over six days and is marked by youths gathering the sacred branches of the lusekwane shrub, a species of acacia, which are then taken to the royal byre to build a small enclosure.

On the third day a bull is ritually slaughtered by the youths. On the fourth day, the King, in full ceremonial dress, joins his warriors in the traditional ncwala dance, after which he enters a special hut within the sacred enclosure. Further rituals ensue, culminating in the King eating the fruits of the new season. As tradition forbids the people to eat the young fruits and vegetables of the season until the King has first tasted them, only when the monarch reappears may his people eat the first fruits with the blessing of the ancestors. The final part of the ceremony is the burning of the King's bedding and household items, thus cleansing everything for the 'new year'. Visitors may not watch 'taboo' sections of the ncwala.

The Umhlanga or Reed Dance

The Umhlanga ceremony takes place annually in late August or early September. It attracts young girls from all over the Kingdom who come to honour and pay homage to the Queen Mother in dance. During the first week the girls gather reeds from specially selected areas to help repair the Queen Mother's home. The day of the Reed Dance begins with the bathing and grooming of the young girls. They wear short beaded skirts decorated with fringes and buttons, necklaces, anklets, bracelets and colourful sashes. The Royal Family Princesses wear red feathers in their hair and lead the girls to perform before their King and Queen Mother.

Religion

The majority of the Swazi people are Christians although many also follow indigenous religious practices. Other belief systems are Islam, Hinduism and Buddhism.

Cuisine

Traditional Swazi food consists mainly of meat, vegetables and porridge. A favourite dish is *igusha*, a type of spinach served with mealie meal. Popular beverages include soft drinks, beer and the local brew *amagano*.

Sport and Leisure Facilities

Numerous sport and leisure pursuits are well catered for within Swaziland. Swazi Trails offers cultural, wildlife and adventure tours. Information is available at tourism information offices or hotel reception desks.

Golf

There are some superb golf courses, with 18-hole courses located at the Royal Swazi Sun and Mbabane Golf Club.

Fishing

Popular venues for fishing include those in the Usutu Forests and Meikles Mount at Mhlambanyati.

Horse Riding

Several riding stables offer out-rides into the surrounding area. The Mlilwane Wildlife Sanctuary offers game viewing on horseback and there are several trails in the Usutu Forests.

White Water River Rafting

The Great Usutu River provides an ideal venue for white water rafting within Swaziland. Trips start at the Sangweni Gate of Mlilwane Wildlife Sanctuary.

Conservation and Eco-Tourism

The foundation of Swaziland's conservation efforts and the re-introduction of extinct species were largely due to the efforts of His Majesty King Sobhuza II and conservationist Ted Reilly. Today, under the direction of His Majesty King Mswati III and the continued efforts of Ted Reilly, the nation's wildlife has grown and the country boasts numerous game and nature reserves.

Wildlife Parks and Nature Reserves

Mkhaya Game Reserve

The 6 250ha Mkhaya Game Reserve (owned by Ted Reilly) is a refuge for endangered species where much work has been done to preserve the black rhino. A large herd of Nguni cattle also has sanctuary here. These animals are descended from the original breed that accompanied the first people to Swaziland.

Activities include game drives and walks, and luxury tented accommodation is available within the reserve.

Malolotja Nature Reserve

The Malolotja Nature Reserve covers an area of 18 000ha of mountain and forest wilderness and two of Swaziland's highest peaks, the Ngwenya and Silotwana mountains, are located within the region. The reserve has some 200 kilometres of hiking trails, ranging from easy walks to strenuous hikes, and is known for its bird life, which includes a breeding colony of bald ibis that can be seen at the Malolotja Falls. Accommodation is available in self-catering cabins as well as a small caravan and camp site.

Mlilwane Wildlife Sanctuary

Situated within the Ezulwini Valley, the 4 500ha Mlilwane Wildlife Sanctuary is home to such species as buffalo, white rhino, hippo, nyala, eland and kudu, as well as a large variety of bird life. There are over 100 kilometres of gravel roads for game viewing, horse-trails, guided game trails and game walks. The 8-km Macobane Trail is a popular self-guided hike that follows the historic aqueduct around the Nyonyane Moutain. Accommodation is available in self-catering cabins and cottages and there is a caravan and camp site.

Hlane Royal National Park

The 30 000ha Hlane Royal National Park is Swaziland's largest game reserve, held in trust for the nation by His Majesty King Mswati III. Situated in the Lowveld savannah region of the country it is home to lion, cheetah, leopard, white rhino and elephant, as well as a variety of species of antelope. Self-catering accommodation is available at the Ndlovu and Bhubesi Camp.

Mlawula Nature Reserve

Located in the rugged countryside around the Lebombo Mountains, the Mlawula Nature Reserve covers an area of some 16 500ha between Lomahaha and the town of Siteki. The reserve houses several rare plant species, as well as game and an abundance of bird life. Camping facilities exist within the reserve.

Mbuluzi Game Reserve

Mbuluzi is situated in the north-eastern bushveld region close to Hlane and Mlawula and has a wide diversity of habitats. It is popular among bird-watchers, with over 300 species recorded within the area. There are several well-marked walking trails throughout the park. Self-catering accommodation is available in the Mbuluzi Game Lodges overlooking the Mlawula River.

Tourist Attractions

Lobamba

Lobamba is the home of the Royal Kraal and the centre of Government within the Kingdom. It is here that the traditional ceremonies of *Ncwala* and *Umhlanga* take place. Situated close to the village is the Swaziland National Museum, exhibiting the country's cultural and natural heritage, Parliament Buildings and Sommhlolo Stadium.

Handicraft Centres

There are numerous handicraft centres found throughout Swaziland that offer beautifully handmade items for sale. Some of the best known outlets are the Ngwenya Glass Factory which produces handmade Ngwenya glass figurines from recycled glass; the Matenga Handicrafts Centre, which sells an array of handmade goods; Swazi Candles and Tishweshwe Crafts which display crafts from the whole of the African continent.

Cultural Village

Swazi Cultural Village

The Swazi Cultural Village is a replica of a mid-nineteenth century homestead. The people of the village demonstrate the Swazi culture through song, dance, story telling, drama, crafting, and the preparation of a conventional Swazi meal. Accommodation is available in traditional beehive-shaped huts just outside the village.

Activity

Draw up a profile of the type of client you would recommend for a holiday in Swaziland and give reasons for your representation.

REPUBLIC OF NAMIBIA

Facts at a Glance

Capital	Windhoek
Size	824 269 sq km
Population	1,6m
Currency	1 Namibian dollar = 100 cents
Average Temperature	Summer min 17°C/max 34°C
– Windhoek	Winter min 6°C/max 22°C
Main Languages	Afrikaans, English, German, Oshivambo, Herero, Nama
Main Religions	Christianity, Indigenous Beliefs
Time Zone	Winter GMT+1 (April – August)
	Summer GMT+2 (September – March)

Geographical Outline

Situated in the south-western part of Africa, the Republic of Namibia borders South Africa to the south and south-east, Botswana to the east, and Angola to the north. The Caprivi Strip extends into the north-eastern part of the country bordering Zambia, Zimbabwe and Botswana, whilst the Atlantic Ocean forms the country's entire western coastline.

The country's perennial rivers include the Kunene, Okavango, Zambezi to the north and east and the Orange to the south, all of which form international boundaries. Mountains located within the country include the Brandberg, the Waterberg, and the Spitzkoppe, known as the 'Matterhorn of Namibia', the Erongo and the Great Karas Mountains.

The topography of the land can be divided into four regions: the Namib Desert and coastal belt; the Central Plateau, on which the nation's capital Windhoek is situated; the southern and eastern Kalahari region which borders Botswana and South Africa; and the wooded bushveld region of the north.

Namibia is home to several interesting species of flora. The *kokerboom* or quiver tree, found in the southern part of the country, was traditionally used by the San for making arrow quivers; the Nara bushes which form large tangles of green spiked stems; and the ancient *Welwitschia mirabilis*, found in the central Namib Desert, reported to be able to live to over one thousand years.

Introduction

The Region

Namibia is fondly referred to as 'Africa's Gem'. It is one of the continent's most recent independent nations, having gained its independence on 21 March 1990.

It is a vast land of stark beauty whose geographical extremes vary from the sand dunes of the Namib Desert to the forests and waterways of the north east. The country has a rich and colourful history and culture evident within its towns and rural areas.

The Economy

The country's natural resources include diamonds, uranium, copper, lead, silver, tungsten, zinc and tin. Much of the population is involved in agriculture, raising cattle and karakul sheep in the central and southern regions and subsistence farming in the northern areas. The nation's fishing industry revolves around the deep-water harbour at Walvis Bay. The waters off its coastline are rich in marine life, which thrive in the cold waters of the Benguela Current.

The Importance of Tourism

Tourism in Namibia is a developing industry, which has much potential. The nation has a good infrastructure with tarred roads connecting all the main centres and a comprehensive air service network.

Traditionally, the majority of Namibia's tourists were from South Africa, mostly driving in their own vehicles, visiting the game parks and taking advantage of recreational activities such as the superb sea fishing. However, this is rapidly changing as the country's stature as a tourist destination grows and more tourists from Europe, North America and the Far East visit its shores.

Climate

Namibia's climate is diverse and depends greatly upon altitude and region. The daytime temperatures in the central Namib regions can climb to over 40°C during the summer months. Winter days are usually warm with clear blue skies, but the temperature falls rapidly at night, with occasional frost. The low-lying areas in the east and north-eastern part of the country are generally hotter than the Central Plateau. In contrast, the coastline that runs parallel to the Namib Desert is kept cool and damp by the cold Benguela Current, which brings a thick coastal fog to its shores. The rainy season extends from October to April.

As the temperatures in certain areas of the country tend to soar to uncomfortable heights during the summer months, some resorts are closed. The best months to visit Namibia are between April and September when temperatures are cooler. Game viewing is also at its best at this time as the animals congregate around the waterholes in the dry season.

Tourism Destinations Southern Africa

Transportation and Accessibility
Road

Despite the well sign-posted tarred roads connecting the main centres, most of the secondary roads are gravel and distances between centres are extensive. Gravel is usually mixed with salt water in the construction of these roads and caution is advised when driving, as the surface can become very slippery in misty weather.

Coaches operate throughout Namibia as well as into South Africa. Various half- and full-day tours are offered from Windhoek and Swakopmund to the surrounding tourist attractions.

Car hire facilities, including four-wheel-drive vehicles, exist in Windhoek and most major centres throughout the country.

Aranos																					
569	Aus
493	134	Bethanie
218	898	822	Gobabis
850	1145	1069	657	Grootfontein
566	346	343	895	1142	Karasburg
581	876	800	388	403	873	Karabib
358	211	157	687	934	208	665	Keetmanshoop
692	125	259	1021	1268	471	999	334	Lüderitz
248	249	257	498	824	540	555	332	374	Maltahöhe
137	432	356	466	713	429	444	221	555	111	Mariental
469	764	688	276	381	761	112	553	889	443	332	Okahandja
642	937	861	449	342	934	61	726	1060	616	505	173	Omaruru
761	1174	980	568	87	1053	404	845	1179	735	624	292	253	Otavi
643	938	862	450	207	935	197	727	1061	617	506	174	135	118	Otjiwarongo
716	1011	935	523	280	1008	269	800	1134	690	579	247	208	191	73	Outjo
311	606	530	292	539	603	270	395	729	285	174	158	331	450	332	405	Rehoboth
1133	1553	1477	1065	494	1550	686	1345	1676	1232	1121	789	750	497	615	688	947	Ruacana
756	1051	975	563	598	1048	175	840	731	482	619	287	236	489	371	444	445	684	Swakopmund
824	1119	1043	631	60	1116	377	907	1242	798	687	355	316	63	181	228	513	434	552	Tsumeb
784	700	708	594	690	1079	206	814	938	451	650	318	267	521	403	476	476	715	31	673	Walvis Bay
395	693	618	205	452	690	181	482	816	372	261	71	242	363	245	318	87	860	356	426	389	Windhoek

▷ *Distances are measured in kilometres*

Border Crossings

There are several border crossings into Namibia.

The main posts are:

Angola: Ruacana (08:00–18:00), Omahenene (08:00–18:00) and Oshikango (08:00–18:00)
Botswana: Buitepos/Mamuno (07:00–19:00) and Mohembo (08:00–18:00)
South Africa: Ariamsvlei and Noordoewer (24 hours), Oranjemund (08:00–17:00), Velloorsdrif (08:00–22:00), Hohlweg (08:00–22:00) and Klein Menasse (08:00–22:00)
Zambia: Wenela (06:00–19:00)
Namibia/Botswana/Zambia/Zimbabwe meet at Kazungula Road (06:00–18:00)

Air

Namibia's national airline, Air Namibia, operates international flights between Windhoek and London/Frankfurt and regionally to South Africa, Botswana, Zimbabwe and Zambia as well as within Namibia. Several other airlines, including South African Airways, serve Namibia through Windhoek International Airport. Many of Namibia's luxury camps have their own airstrip.

Rail

There is a limited rail network that connects Windhoek with the country's main centres.

The Desert Express train offers a 24-hour excursion in five-star comfort from Windhoek to Swakopmund, stopping at various points en route, and the Shongololo Express offers a fully serviced tour of Namibia, which travels overnight, arriving at a new destination each morning.

Visa Requirements

Visitors to Namibia require a valid passport. Information on visa requirements can be obtained from the Ministry of Home Affairs in Windhoek, the Namibian Embassy or Namibia Tourist Office. Most nationalities, including South Africans, Americans and British citizens, do not require a visa to enter the country.

Accommodation

Namibia has a large variety of accommodation options to suit every budget. There are numerous luxury hotels, lodges and tented camps to be found in the popular tourist destinations, Resort complexes exist throughout the country, as do small hotels, guesthouses, guest farms, bed and breakfast facilities, backpacker establishments, and caravan and camp sites.

Most types of accommodation within Namibia are graded using a star system – regular inspections are carried out by the Ministry of Wildlife Conservation and Tourism.

Health

Precaution against malaria is advisable in the northern parts of the country (including Etosha) and bilharzia is prevalent in most rivers.

Historic Highlights

Nambia was first inhabited by the San and later the Khoikhoi from the south.

Evidence suggests that the first groups of people from the north arrived in the region some 2 400 years ago.

During the 19th century Germany annexed the country, except for Walvis Bay which was taken as part of the Cape Colony.

In 1904, a rebellion of the Herero left many of the nation's people dead.

German colonial rule came to an end during World War I when the South African army, fighting for the Allied Forces, defeated the Germans.

At the end of World War I, the League of Nations gave South Africa the mandate to rule what was then known as South West Africa. Despite a United Nations (UN) decision in 1966 to terminate the mandate, South Africa continued to rule the country, which culminated in a lengthy war between SWAPO (South West Africa Peoples' Organisation) and South Africa.

UN-monitored elections were held in 1989 and independence was granted in 1990 under the presidency of Sam Nujoma.

Population

Nambia has one of the lowest population densities in Africa. The largest group is the Ovambo. Other significant groups include the Herero, Himba, Kavango, Caprivians, Damara, Nama, Basters, San, and people of German and Afrikaner descent.

▷ *Herero woman in traditional dress*

Social and Cultural Profile

The diversity of the ethnic groups who live in Namibia has had a significant impact on the nation's culture. Many of the people are involved in stock farming, subsistence farming and other pastoral pursuits.

The German influence is apparent in the country's architecture, language and food, with many types of typically Germanic breads, sausages and confectionery found in the local shops.

Religion

Most Namibians are Christians of various Protestant denominations, but there is also a substantial Roman Catholic population, especially in the central and northern regions. A small minority of Namibia's people, mostly among the Himba and San, continue to practise their traditional form of religion. However, many indigenous religious practices have been incorporated into their Christian beliefs.

Cuisine

The typical Nambian-style cuisine includes local game such as gemsbok, kudu, springbok, ostrich steaks, as well as beef and mutton. Seafood specialities include rock lobster, oysters, kingklip and sole. The Germanic influence is also evident in the large selection of traditional sausage and polony, breads, mouth-watering cakes and pastries, as well as typical dishes such as eisbein or kassler with sauerkraut.

The local beer is brewed according to the traditional Reinheitsgebot (purity laws) issued by the Duke of Bavaria (Germany) in 1516 and only natural ingredients are used.

Traditional food includes *mieliepap* (maize porridge), or *mahango* made from millet, which is eaten with fish or meat stew, pumpkin, gem squash and butternut, as well as milk products such as curds. Popular brews include *mataku* – a wine made from watermelon, and *walende* – a spirit distilled from the palm.

Festivals and Events

Popular festivals and events include Independence Day on 21 March; Maherero Day towards the end of August when the Herero people gather at Okahandja, north of Windhoek; the WIKA or Windhoek Karnival held in March/April; the Kuska Karnival held in Swakopmund in August; and the Oktoberfest.

Sport and Leisure Facilities

Sport in Namibia, as in most of its neighbouring countries, is an integral part of life. Popular sports include rugby, soccer and athletics. Outdoor activities such as hiking, mountaineering, angling and hunting are also popular pastimes.

Hiking

The country has great walking and hiking possibilities. Permits and a doctor's fitness certificate are usually required for multi-day walks, such as those in the Fish River Canyon, Waterberg Plateau and Naukluft Mountains.

Fishing

Fishing enthusiasts have plenty of choice areas along the Namib coastline. Excellent rock and surf fishing exists from Swakopmund to the Ugab River, in the National West Coast Tourist Recreation Area.

Horse Riding

Horse riding is a popular pastime and organised treks are available at several locations. Information is available at tourist information offices.

Hunting

Namibia is a very popular venue for hunting safaris. Laws are very strict – participants have to be accompanied by a professional hunter or a registered guide.

Hot-Air Ballooning

A hot-air balloon ride over the Sossusvlei, followed by a champagne breakfast, is a favourite activity of visitors to the area.

Conservation and Eco-Tourism

Namibia was the first country in the world to include in its constitution the protection of the environment and sustainable utilisation of wildlife. Over 15 per cent of the country has been set aside as national parks, protecting and preserving the nation's endangered flora and fauna.

Community tourism projects are being carried out throughout Namibia by various organisations in areas such as the Damaraland Camp, where the local people are actively involved in the protection and management of the land and wildlife.

The Etosha National Park provides a sanctuary for four rare and endangered species – the black rhino, the black-faced impala, Damara dik-dik, and the Hartmann's mountain zebra.

Wildlife Parks and Nature Reserves

Etosha National Park

The Etosha National Park was proclaimed a game reserve by German Governor von Linequist in 1907 and covers an area of 22 270 sq km. It is centred round an extensive flat saline depression of about 5 000 sq km, known as the Etosha Pan, and is considered to be one of Africa's great game parks.

The park accommodates over 144 mammal species, which include the world's largest concentration of black rhino, as well as elephant, lion, cheetah, leopard, large numbers of gemsbok, springbok, Burchell's zebra and wildebeest. There is also abundant bird life, including the nation's national bird, the crimson-breasted shrike.

There are three rest camps situated within the park – Okaukuejo, Halali and Namutoni. Fort Namutoni was once the headquarters of the colonial troops of Imperial Germany. Each camp has floodlit waterholes enabling guests to view game without having to leave the camp. Facilities include self-catering bungalow-style accommodation, caravan and camp sites, a swimming pool, restaurant, shop and a petrol station.

Several luxury lodges have been developed in the vicinity of the park, including Mokuti Lodge, Ongava Lodge, and Etosha Aoba Lodge.

Namib-Naukluft Park

The Namib–Naukluft Park covers an area of around 49 768 sq km and is the largest nature conservation area in Namibia. Its diverse landscape ranges from desert plains and high dunes, to deep gorges and an estuarine lagoon. Due to its size, the park is split into various sections – Welwitschia Drive, the Naukluft, Sesriem and Sossusvlei, Sandwich Harbour and the northern section between the Kuiseb and Swakop rivers.

Welwitschia Drive

The Welwitschia Drive is situated in the northern part of the park and takes you through vast plains where oryx, zebra and springbok roam. The *Welwitschia mirabilis*, a famous desert plant, is found along the way.

Naukluft

The Naukluft is situated on the road towards Swakopmund and incorporates the mountainous escarpment and edge of the Namib Desert. It is a sanctuary for rare Hartmann's mountain zebra and several day hikes are to be found within the area as well as a campsite and several guest farms.

Sesriem and Sossusvlei

The Sesriem and Sossusvlei area is a popular and much photographed region of the park. The dunes at Sossusvlei rise up to 300m and are tinted in every possible shade from pale apricot to vivid red. Popular excursions offered at Sossusvlei include 4x4 dune drives into the desert, and hot-air balloon rides.

▷ *The dunes at Sossusvlei*

Sandwich Harbour

Sandwich Harbour is well known for its prolific bird life and several species migrate annually to this wetland area. Thousands of flamingos, sandpipers and terns are to be found in the lagoon and mud flats of the region.

Northern Section

The region between the Kuiseb and Swakop rivers is a region of rocky plains bisected by the Swakop River Valley.

National West Coast Tourist Recreation Area

Stretching some 200km from Swakopmund to the Ugab River, the National West Coast Tourist Recreation Area offers excellent rock and surf fishing. The resort of Henties Bay, located within the region, has a varied choice of accommodation. To the north of the bay lies a large colony of Cape Fur Seals at the Cape Cross Seal Reserve.

Skeleton Coast Park

The park covers an area of some 1 500 000ha from the Ugab River to the Kunene River on the Angolan border. Other than a number of birds and desert animals, several shipwrecks and abandoned mines, this fog-bound stretch of coastline is desolate. The southern region of the park has two small fishing resorts at Terrace Bay and Torra Bay. The northern section, the Skeleton Coast Park Wilderness Area, stretches from the Hoanib River to the Angolan border and is only accessible by means of fly-in safaris.

Private Game Reserves

Several private game reserves are to be found throughout the country, offering luxury accommodation and a variety of activities such as night drives, game walks and horseback safaris. Information is available at the tourist information offices.

Tourist Attractions

Northern Region

Caprivi

The Caprivi is a long thin stretch of land lying in the north-eastern part of the country bordering Botswana, Zambia and Angola. It is a region of woodlands and wetlands, cut by several rivers including the Kwando, Chobe, Okavango and Zambezi. The area boasts several safari lodges offering activities such as fishing, hiking, river-trips and game safaris. The Caprivi Art Centre at Katima Mulilo displays the distinctive woodcarving, pottery and basketry of the region.

Kaokoland

Situated in the north-western part of the country is the harsh and rugged wilderness region of Kaokoland, an area best negotiated by four-wheel-drive vehicles. The exception to this barren landscape is the area around the Kunene River and Epupa Falls where the land is transformed into a lush riverine wilderness – a popular walking and hiking area, with a wealth of bird life. There is a small luxury tented camp situated on the banks of the river just to the east of the falls which can be reached by light aircraft or four-wheel-drive vehicles.

Damaraland

There are several attractions worth visiting in the Damaraland region. To the west of Khorixas is the Petrified Forest, where fossilised tree trunks may be seen, as well as the nearby rock formations known as the Organ Pipes, and the Stone Age rock engravings at Twyfelfontein. To the south of Twyfelfontein rise the imposing slopes of Namibia's highest mountain, the Brandberg, known for its wealth of rock paintings which includes the famous 'White Lady' found on the north-eastern side of the mountain.

Central Region

Windhoek

Set in Namibia's Central Highlands region, Windhoek is the nation's capital. The German influence is evident throughout the city in its architecture, restaurants and coffee shops. Places worth visiting include the Tintenpalast – now the National Assembly building; the Christuskirche; the Alte Feste which has been transformed into a museum; the Namibia Crafts Centre; and the Transnamib Railway Station and Museum. The Hofmeyer Walk, which begins in the city, takes visitors into the nearby Klein Windhoek Valley.

▷ *The bronze cavalryman looks towards the Christuskirche*

Accommodation within the city varies from luxury hotels to small Germanic guesthouses. There are several resorts in the vicinity, offering recreational facilities such as hiking trails, birding, angling and swimming.

Swakopmund

The small seaside town of Swakopmund lies to the north of Walvis Bay at the mouth of the Swakop River. Nestled between the desert and the ocean, the town has retained much of its German colonial atmosphere and charm. The town has several tourist attractions in close proximity, including the Swakopmund Museum and tours into the Namib.

Tourism Destinations Southern Africa

Walvis Bay

Walvis Bay is Namibia's only deep-water harbour and is the nation's main port. Once used by whalers and guano collectors, the bay is now the hub of the country's expanding fishing industry.

One of the town's most striking sights is the large number of birds that frequent its lagoon. Several species of migratory birds – terns, chestnut-banded plovers and sandpipers – as well as about half of southern Africa's flamingos are to be found in the area.

Duwisib Castle

Duwisib Castle bears testimony to a bygone era in the history of Namibia when people of European descent came to the land and built huge mansions in the desert. The castle, situated on the edge of the Namib Desert, was built by a German aristocrat, Baron Hansheinrich Von Wolff.

Southern Region

Luderitz

The remote town of Luderitz lies in the southern part of Namibia. Once a busy port and mining centre, the town has also retained much of its German character. Attractions include the museum, which has exhibits on the history and people of Luderitz as well as its diamond-mining industry, and the Felsenkirche known for its beautiful stained-glass windows. The coastline and beaches are home to flocks of flamingo, colonies of penguins and seals. Trips to the Cape Fur Seal Sanctuary depart from the harbour daily. Another attraction to be found within the area is the 'ghost mining town' of Kolmanskop, which is returning to the desert.

Fish River Canyon

One of the country's most popular destinations, the awe-inspiring Fish River Canyon, is a 161km long and 27km wide ravine carved through ancient rock formations and surrounded by high cliffs. A road runs for some 25km along its eastern edge leading to several viewing sites.

Fish River Canyon Hiking Trail

The canyon's popular five-day hiking trail begins from the main lookout point and terminates at the Ai-Ais hot springs resort. The hike is open between May and September and a medical certificate of fitness is required.

Ai-Ais

Situated in the southern end of the Fish River Canyon, Ai-Ais is a well-established hot spring resort. The spring waters bubble to the surface at a temperature of 60°C and are piped into Jacuzzis and swimming pools. The resort is closed from November to mid-March when the Fish River is known to rage through the canyon. Accommodation ranges from luxury apartments to a caravan and camp site.

Kalkfeld

There is evidence in the sandstone, some 29km from Kalkfeld, that dinosaurs roamed the region – three-toed prints embedded in the once wet sand of an ancient lake, are now petrified stone.

Activity

Describe the type of client to whom you would recommend Namibia as a holiday destination, giving reasons for your representation.

REPUBLIC OF BOTSWANA

Facts at a Glance

Capital	Gaborone
Size	582 000 sq km
Population	1,4m
Currency	1 pula = 100 thebe
Average Temperature	Summer min 20°C/max 33°C
– Gaborone	Winter min 4°C/max 23°C
Main Languages	seTswana, seKalanga, English
Main Religions	Christianity, Indigenous Beliefs
Time Zone	GMT+2

Geographical Outline

The landlocked country of Botswana is bounded to the north and west by Namibia, to the north-east by Zimbabwe and along its south-eastern and southern border by South Africa. In the north-eastern extremity of the country, Botswana shares the world's shortest border of 700m with Zambia.

The vast Kalahari Desert covers some 84 per cent of the land. The country's vegetation consists mainly of savannah grassland, dotted with acacia, thorn bush and scrub. The exceptions to the typical savannah terrain lie in the north-east where deciduous forests are found, and in the north-western area where the country's only perennial river, the Okavango, transforms the landscape into the lush, verdant region of the Okavango Delta. The south-eastern part of the country has the greatest rainfall and agricultural potential as well as the highest population density.

Several of the region's rivers serve as national boundaries. The Chobe River runs between Botswana and Namibia's Caprivi Strip, the Limpopo and Molopo form part of the border with South Africa, and the Zambezi marks the spot where four countries – Botswana, Namibia, Zimbabwe and Zambia – meet at Kazungula. The Okavango flows into the north-western part of the country from the eastern Angolan Highlands to form the world's largest inland delta, before drying up in the desert sands.

There are no mountains in Botswana, only hills. However, ranges such as the Tsodilo, Aha and Gcwihaba Hills are of significant geological and historical importance.

Introduction

The Region

Botswana has a wealth of wildlife parks and nature reserves covering a wide variety of habitats and offering visitors a chance to experience true African wilderness.

The Economy

Shortly after Independence in 1967, diamond mines were discovered within Botswana. Today, the nation enjoys one of the highest growth rates of GNP per capita in the world and has one of the world's fastest growing economies. Its stable political climate and natural resources assist in making its currency, the pula, one of Africa's strongest currencies.

Agriculture plays an important role in the country, with the majority of its people, especially in the rural areas, being involved in either livestock farming or subsistence farming.

The Importance of Tourism

Tourism plays an important role in Botswana and is a significant earner of foreign exchange. Recent moves have seen a change in direction from 'trophy hunting' to photographic safaris and eco-tourism. The industry provides a fairly substantial portion of formal employment and is considered to be a major growth industry. In an effort to preserve the natural environment, government policy has been one of low-volume, high-cost tourism and it is consequently an expensive tourism destination, catering for upmarket visitors, with little or no accommodation possibilities in certain areas for budget travellers.

Climate

The summer months (October–April) can be fairly hot and there is a good possibility of afternoon thundershowers. Winter days are usually warm, clear and sunny, with temperatures dropping fairly dramatically at night. The rainy season is generally from November to March. Although two-thirds of the country lies within the tropics, the whole region is mostly dry and prone to drought.

Transportation and Accessibility

Road

There is a fairly limited road network within Botswana but many roads are being developed or upgraded. Main roads connect the nation's important centres and secondary roads serve remote areas. Roads connect from South Africa and Zimbabwe to the main Gaborone–Francistown–Chobe route. From Francistown there is a fully tarred road to Maun via the northern edge of the Makgadikgadi Pans, joining up with the road that skirts the Okavango Delta and continuing up to Sepupa and the Tsodilo Hills region. Connections between Sehitwa and Ghanzi and

Tourism Destinations Southern Africa

Takatshwaane in the Kalahari region link up with the artery across the south-western part of the country via Lokalane, Kang, Sekoma, Jwaneng and Kanye. At Kanye the road forks to Gaborone and Lobatse on the South African border. Many of the region's secondary roads become impassable during the rainy season.

Buses operate between Gaborone and Johannesburg, between Gaborone and Harare via Francistown, and between Bulawayo, Kasane and Victoria Falls, and Livingstone. The Trans-Namib bus runs between Ghanzi and Gobabis in Namibia.

Branches of a well-known car hire company can be found in most main centres throughout Botswana.

Bokspits																					
1156	Francistown																				
874	433	Gaborone																			
724	778	712	Ghanzi																		
591	629	202	519	Jwaneng																	
591	871	438	274	240	Kang																
645	547	120	592	82	319	Kanye															
1755	488	909	933	1122	1152	1029	Kasane														
1747	480	921	920	1109	1245	1041	12	Kazangula													
649	508	75	637	127	363	45	1008	996	Lobatse												
921	235	198	1013	400	636	318	735	723	273	Mahalapye											
1151	492	915	286	801	560	1035	616	604	990	717	Maun										
1455	188	621	590	817	865	741	312	300	690	417	304	Nata									
1397	240	673	1010	864	1110	792	732	720	748	475	724	420	Orapa								
1000	163	270	941	471	708	390	663	651	345	72	655	351	403	Palapye							
697	556	123	685	175	411	93	1056	1044	48	321	1048	744	796	393	Ramatiabama						
1239	82	515	860	711	953	635	582	570	590	317	574	270	322	380	638	Ramokgwebama					
1134	151	402	929	605	840	522	651	639	477	204	643	339	391	132	525	233	Selebi-Phikwe				
1046	210	315	988	517	747	429	709	697	384	111	702	398	450	47	432	292	179	Serowe			
1046	84	342	869	545	780	462	585	572	417	144	583	279	324	72	465	164	60	119	Serule		
246	910	478	619	333	345	399	1411	1399	410	676	905	1099	1151	748	451	993	888	800	828	Tshabong	
381	777	350	491	198	217	283	1283	1271	275	548	777	965	1017	620	323	865	754	666	693	128	Werda

▷ *Distances are measured in kilometres*

Border Crossings

The main border crossings into Botswana are as follows:

Namibia: Mohembo (06:00–19:00), Buitepos/Mamuno – the Trans-Kalahari Highway (07:00–19:00)

South Africa: Ramatlabama (07:00–20:00), Kopfontein (07:00–22:00), Derdepoort (07:00–19:00), Swartkopfonteinhek (07:00–19:00), Stockpoort (08:00–18:00), Groblersbrug (08:00–18:00)

Zimbabwe: Ramokawebana Road (06:00–20:00)

Botswana/Namibia/Zambia/Zimbabwe meet at Kazungula (06:00–18:00)

Air

International Airports are located in Gaborone, Maun and Kasane. Air Botswana operates regular flights between Johannesburg, Harare, Windhoek, Francistown, Maun and Kasane. British Airways has a regular service between London and Gaborone, and SAA operates between Gaborone and Johannesburg. Several air charter companies operate out of Gaborone and Maun.

Rail

There is a train service that operates between Lobatse, Gaborone and Francistown.

Visa Requirements

Most visitors to Botswana, including South African, British and American passport holders, do not require a visa for visits up to 90 days.

Accommodation

Although no hotel grading system operates within Botswana, several luxury hotels are situated in the capital, including the Gaborone Sun and Grand Palm Hotel, which both have a large casino and entertainment centre. There are also numerous mid-range and budget alternatives.

Accommodation in the wilderness area ranges from upmarket luxury lodges to basic camping facilities. Due to the rough terrain in certain areas, caravans are not well catered for throughout Botswana.

In the remote rural areas where no designated campsites exist, it is customary to ask permission from the local chief before setting up camp on the land.

Historic Highlights

The San are believed to have lived in Botswana since the Middle Stone Age. They maintained their traditional lifestyle until fairly recently by retreating into the remote regions of the country.

Evidence suggests that the people from the north had settled in the region near Palapye a thousand years ago, and by AD1200 a greater power had established itself on Mapungubwe Hill, where the Shashe meets the Limpopo River at the present-day Mashatu Game Reserve.

The *Difaqane* (or *Mfecane*)Wars swept across much of Botswana during the 1800s, when Shaka's opponents fled northwards.

Christianity came to Botswana through the work of the London Missionary Society when Robert Moffat set up a mission station at Kuruman in 1821.

Explorers and traders arrived and ivory became an important commodity bringing wealth to the local people. In 1866 gold was discovered near Francistown.

Botswana became the British Bechuanaland Protectorate in 1885. In 1895 three Tswana Kings – Khama, Bathoen and Sebele – travelled to England to appeal to the government not to transfer the Protectorate to Rhodes and the British South Africa Company. Support came only after the failed Jameson Raid at the end of 1895 when the British government secured the nation's future as a Protectorate. The nation's sovereignty was once again under threat in 1910 after the consolidation of the Union of South Africa, but its protectorate status was upheld until 1966 when the nation gained full Independence from Britain.

In 1966 Sir Seretse Khama was installed as the nation's first president. Although he is now deceased, his party, the Botswana Democratic Party, has governed the country since Independence.

In 1967 diamonds were discovered in Botswana, transforming the country into one of Africa's richest nations.

Health

Precautions against malaria are necessary within Botswana especially during the rainy season from October to May. Tick bite fever is a problem in certain areas and parts of Ngamiland are infested with tsetse fly. Insect repellent, long trousers and socks are a good deterrent. Water is safe to drink in urban areas and most tourist lodges and camps but should be boiled beforehand in rural areas.

Population

The people of Botswana are made up of numerous different groups from diverse backgrounds. The name Batswana refers to anyone of Botswana nationality, regardless of origin. The nation's largest group is the Tswana, which makes up around 50 per cent of the population. The Kalanga, Yei, Subiya and Mbukushu, Kgalagadi, San, Herero, and people of European descent, account for the balance.

Social and Cultural Profile

Batswana are considered to be fairly relaxed and tolerant and their country is one of the most peaceful in Africa.

The Tswana group are traditionally pastoral farmers who live in large villages of up to 30 000 people. They farm both crops and cattle whereas other groups practise subsistence farming or fishing and hunting.

A substantial number of families of European lineage live in Botswana.

Traditional Crafts

Basketry

One of the best known of Botswana's handicrafts is basketry. Made in and around the Okavango Delta, baskets are woven from the mokolane palm and dyed with natural colours. They have a surprising variety of patterns that are representative of different aspects of local life. The designs are given beautifully descriptive names such as Flight of the Swallow, Tears of the Giraffe and The Running Ostrich.

Tourism Destinations Southern Africa

Wall Hangings and Tapestries

Original wall hangings and tapestries are made in the south-eastern region of the country around the villages of Odi and Lobatse.

Woodcarving

Items carved from wood have long been a part of Botswana's traditional handicrafts. Figurines and household items such as spoons and bowls are found throughout the country.

San Handicrafts

The San people of western Botswana create seed-and-bead necklaces and bracelets.

Pottery

Pottery has long been a form of art practised in Botswana and modern potters still use many original designs and patterns to enhance their work.

Literature

Much of the ancient myths and poetry of the indigenous peoples of Botswana has only recently been transcribed. Important books which depict images of life in Botswana include South African born Bessie Head's book on traditional village life, *Serowe – Village of the Rain Wind* and Laurens van der Post's *Lost World of the Kalahari*, on the San people of the Kalahari.

Music and Dance

Music and Dance has been a part of life in Botswana since the time of the San, and traditional dancing accompanied by drums is still popular in the villages and performed at many social events.

The following excerpt exemplifies the San's love of music and dance:

> ... we found this love of music was not peculiar to our own close group but characteristic of all these people in the desert, bearing out the tradition of the Bushman's skill as a musician and his deep devotion to

music ... We concluded music was as vital as water, food and fire to them ... And all their music, song, sense of rhythm, and movement achieved its greatest expression in their dancing.

Excerpt from *Lost World of the Kalahari*
by Laurens van der Post

Language

The national language of Botswana is seTswana, which is spoken by the majority in the country. English is the official business language and is widely spoken throughout the region.

Religion

Christianity is the official religion of Botswana and is practised by the majority of its people. Certain traditional beliefs however, have been incorporated into their form of Christianity.

Cuisine

Most of Botswana's luxury hotels and lodges offer their guests a variety of fine international dishes and there are various fast-food outlets in its cities and towns.

Important ingredients in the local cuisine include millet and sorghum porridge, maize (mealies/corn), beef and milk. The people tend to eat what is plentiful in their region, for example the Yei of the Okavango eat fish, the Kalanga, mainly sorghum, millet and maize, and the Herero, dairy products. Popular dishes include *seswaa*, a beef dish usually served with maize-meal, and the underground tuber known as *morama*, or Kalahari truffle, is eaten in the remote areas. Almost all local groups have food taboos which are practised mostly in the rural areas. Favourite drinks include palm wine and *chibuku*.

Festivals and Events

Important festivals and events which are celebrated in Botswana include New Year's Day, Easter, Ascension Day, President's Day in July, Independence Day on 30 September and the Christmas Season on 25, 26 and 27 December.

Sport and Leisure Facilities

Most visitors to Botswana come to enjoy the spectacular wildlife experience the country has to offer. Options range from bush walks, horse riding safaris, hiking, fishing, mokoro (canoe) rides, boat trips, game drives, and elephant riding safaris. At Gweta Rest Camp and Jack's Camp in the Makgadikgadi Pans area, four-wheel all-terrain bike safaris are available.

Conservation and Eco-Tourism

Much conservation work is being carried out in areas such as the Tuli Block, the Central Kalahari, at Nata on the north-eastern edge of the Sowa Pan where a sanctuary is providing an important breeding ground for pelicans and flamingos, and at the Khama Rhino Sanctuary at Serowe.

Wildlife Parks and Nature Reserves

Okavango Delta

The Okavango Delta is one of Botswana's main tourism destinations. Covering an area of more than 15 000 sq km of lush verdant wetlands, criss-crossed by a multitude of waterways, the region is rich in animal and bird life. One of the best ways of exploring the waterways is by mokoro (a dugout canoe made from a hollowed tree trunk). The canoe is guided through by expert polers.

Numerous upmarket, luxurious safari camps operate here. The region has beautiful lagoons, forested islands and large areas of grassland. Many of the camps can only be reached by light aircraft, giving the Okavango Delta an intimate and secluded atmosphere. Popular resorts include Jedibe Island Camp, Mombo Camp, Pom Pom and Xigera. Activities in the camps include game walks, mokoro rides and fishing.

▷ *Visitors enjoying a mokoro ride*

Maun

Maun is the departure point for flights and overland tours into the Okavango Delta and the headquarters of most safari and air charter companies. The town is the major supplier of everything needed for overland trips and vacationing in the region and has several shopping centres, car and four-wheel-drive hire facilities, hotels and lodges.

Moremi Wildlife Reserve

The Moremi Game Reserve is situated in the north-eastern section of the Delta some 95km by road from Maun. It is accessible by four-wheel-drive vehicle or by air. The park is a prime conservation area, considered to be one of the most beautiful in Africa and has a wide diversity of wildlife and over 400 bird species. The terrain consists of broad channels and lagoons, flood plains, forested islands, mopane woodlands and grasslands. Within the reserve there are four public campsites – South Gate, Third Bridge, Xakanaxa Lagoon and North Gate.

Abu Camp

Abu Camp is a 30-minute flight over the Delta from Maun. The camp specialises in a 6-day, 5-night elephant-back safari package, offering its guests the unique opportunity of spending some time with an elephant family whilst experiencing the African bush. The camp is named after the famous elephant Abu, who featured in films such as *The Power of One* and *White Hunter Black Heart*. He leads a family of 14 elephants.

The lodge itself is set in an ancient riverine forest and consists of five custom-built tents with en-suite bathrooms.

Chobe National Park

The Chobe National Park covers an area of 11 700 sq km of diverse habitat which is home to one of the greatest concentrations of game in southern Africa. The seasonal availability of water precipitates the annual zebra migration across this vast expanse when tens of thousands of animals move over the land. The dry season also brings vast herds of buffalo and elephant to the river's edge. During the summer months the region can become extremely hot and rains can make the roads in the southern and central area impassable. The winter months (the dry season) are often considered to be the best time to visit the area.

Tourism Destinations Southern Africa

Accommodation in the region consists of National Park campsites at Serondela, Buffalo Ridge, Nogatsaa, Tchinga and Linyanti and numerous private lodges and camps.

Chobe can be divided into four distinct areas – the Chobe River Front, the central area around Nogatsaa, Linyanti, and Savuti.

▷ *An elephant and lionesses in Chobe National Park*

Chobe River Front

The road along the riverfront loops to follow the river floodplains, enabling superb game viewing. Private lodges in the area include the Chobe Chilwero Lodge and the Chobe Game Lodge.

Nogatsaa and Tchinga

Nogatsaa and Tchinga are situated some 70km south of Serondela and are considered to be one of the region's best game-viewing areas.

Linyanti

Situated in the corner of the park, the Linyanti Swamp has an abundance of wildlife and a large variety of birds. Lodges in the region include James' Camp, King's Pool, Linyanti and Selinda Camp.

Savuti

One of the most popular areas of the park is Savuti. Wildlife in this region is renowned, with sightings of some of the more elusive species, such as leopard, wild dog and cheetah, fairly common. The annual zebra migration between Linyanti and Savuti brings zebra to the region in late November where they foal. The area is also known for its San rock art and there are several sites to be found in the region's rocky hills.

Accommodation at Savuti includes Allan's Camp, Savuti South (sister camp to Allan's Camp), and Lloyd's Camp.

Central Kalahari Game Reserve

The Central Kalahari Game Reserve was established in 1961 and covers a region of 52 800 sq km. The area was originally set aside as the last domain of the nomadic San. Camping is permitted at Piper's and Sunday Pan in Deception Valley in the northern part of the park. However, there is no drinking water or other facilities at these sites and the only camp at the reserve where drinking water is available, is at the Game Scout Camp at Matswere in the south-eastern region of the park.

Gemsbok National Park/
Kgalagadi Transfrontier Park (KTP)

In the remote south-western region of Botswana, adjacent to South Africa's Kalahari Gemsbok National Park, lies the Gemsbok National Park. The park was established in 1937 to protect the environment and preserve the region's large herds of wildlife. The park, together with the Kalahari Gemsbok National Park in South Africa, has recently become southern Africa's first formal transfrontier conservation area. On 7 April 1999, the presidents of Botswana and South Africa signed a historic treaty linking the two parks. The park has been renamed the Kgalagadi Transfrontier Park (KTP) and covers and area of 7 991 sq km.

Makgadikgadi Pans

The Makgadikgadi Pans are on a flat barren expanse covering an area of 12 000 sq km. The pans are the remains of a great lake that once covered most of Botswana. After the first rains, the pans are transformed with water and fresh grass, and thousands of grazers descend upon the area along with stalking predators and massive flocks of water birds. Much evidence of ancient settlements has been found around the Makgadikgadi, including several sites on the shores of southern Sowa.

The three main pans of the region are the Nxai Pan, the Sowa Pan, and the Ntwetwe Pan. The region is best suited to four-wheel-drive vehicles, and aircraft landing strips exist at Nata and Gweta.

The Makgadikgadi and Nxai Pan National Park

The Makgadikgadi and Nxai Pan National Park covers an area of just under 7 500 sq km. The park has no hotels or lodges, only designated campsites, and visitors must either be part of an organised safari or self-sufficient.

The landscape is dotted with large baobab trees, used for navigation purposes by the early explorers of the region. The most famous is the cluster known as Baines' Baobabs. These trees, immortalised by the painter Thomas Baines who painted them during his expedition in 1862, are situated close to the Kudiakam Pan and are a popular picnic spot.

▷ *Baines' Baobabs*

Nxai Pan

The Nxai Pan is covered in short grass, which attracts large herds of grazers to the region, as well as lion, leopard and hyena.

There are two campsites at Nxai Pan – South Camp on the edge of Nxai and North Camp at the top end. Both camps have running water and braai (barbecue) facilities.

Ntwetwe Pan

Since the waters of the Boteti River which once fed the pan have been diverted at Mopipi Dam, the region is almost permanently dry.

Sowa Pan

During the wet season the vast white expanse of the Sowa Pan is home to flocks of water-loving birds, including the pelican and thousands of greater and lesser flamingos. The southern region of the pan is dotted with several granite islands. The most famous of these is Kubu Island, an area of huge granite boulders, age-old baobabs and the remains of an ancient settlement.

Popular private camps to be found within the Makgadikgadi region include Gweta Camp and Jack's Camp:

Gweta Camp

Facilities at Gweta comprise chalets, a swimming pool, restaurant, bar and curio shop. Activities offered at the camp are guided horse trails, quad-bike trips and overnight trips onto the pans.

Jack's Camp

Jack's Camp is situated between Gweta and the Makgadikgadi and Nxai Pan National Park on the edge of the Ntwetwe Pan. Quad-bike trips into the surrounding area are also available from Jack's Camp.

Eastern Botswana and the Tuli Block

The eastern part of the country receives higher rainfall than the rest of the land and is a region of commercial farmland and privately owned game conservation sectors. Several private game reserves have been established in this area which has resulted in the creation of the North-East Tuli Game Reserve which covers the region north of the Motloutse River. The area is becoming an important eco-tourism destination where many conservation projects are being carried out.

Mashatu Game Reserve

Occupying the area between the Shashe and Limpopo rivers, the Mashatu Game Reserve covers some 46 000ha of pristine land. The region boasts one of the world's largest elephant populations on private land, and over 350 different species of bird. The reserve offers game viewing walks and night drives.

Accommodation is available at the Majale Lodge and Thakadu Tented Camp.

Tuli Game Reserve

The Tuli Game Reserve is situated in about 7 500ha of land adjacent to the Mashatu Game Reserve. Accommodation consists of the Tuli Safari Lodge and Nokalodi Tented Camp.

Tourist Attractions

Gaborone

Gaborone is the capital of Botswana and is one of Africa's fastest growing cities. Situated in the south-eastern corner of the country, the city is the main point of entry into Botswana for tourists. There is a good selection of hotels and entertainment venues. Places of interest include the National Museum and Art Gallery, which houses some original works by the famous artist Thomas Baines, and the nearby Gaborone and Mokolodi Game Reserves.

Places worth visiting along the Gaborone–Francistown road include the silting ponds situated near Phakalane – a protected wetland area with a large population of flamingos and other water birds; the village of Odi where attractive woven products can be seen; the cultural village of Mochudi, well known for its local arts and crafts, and the Phuthadikobo Museum, which details the Bakgatla people.

Francistown

Francistown is one of Botswana's oldest towns and is capital of the North. The town's museum exhibits the history and heritage of the local people.

Serowe

Serowe has been the capital of the Ngwato district since King Khama III moved from Phalatswe in 1902. It is one of sub-Saharan Africa's largest villages. The history of the village is linked to that of the country's first President, Seretse Khama, nephew of Tshekedi Khama and heir to the Ngwato throne. Whilst studying law in London he met and married an Englishwoman, Ruth Williams. He was expected to marry within the Tswana royal family and was consequently stripped of his inheritance and exiled from his native land. In 1956 he renounced his rights to the Ngwato throne and was permitted to return to Serowe where a campaign was begun for Botswana's Independence. When Independence was granted to the nation, Seretse Khama became Botswana's first President.

Places of interest in the village include the Khama III Memorial Museum, which contains the history of Serowe and the Khama family.

Tsodilo Hills

Located in the north-western region of Botswana, the Tsodilo Hills are considered to be one of the world's most significant rock art sites, with some 3 500 paintings spanning over 25 000 years of human habitation in the region.

▷ *San rock art*

Aha and Gcwihaba Hills

The Aha and Gcwihaba Hills are located about 150km south of Tsodilo. The Drotsky's or Gcwihaba Caverns found in the area are filled with magnificent stalagmites, stalactites and flowstone formations.

Livingstone Memorial

Situated some 40km from Gaborone along the Kanye Road are the ruins of David Livingstone's house and mission, built during the 1840s. The church was the first in Botswana and was where Chief Sechele was converted to Christianity.

Activity

Match the destination with the client's requirements.

Client's Requirement	*Destination*
Elephant-back safaris	Makgadikgadi Pans
Quad bike outings	Okavango Delta
Mokoro rides	Savuti
Sightings of wild dog	Abu Camp
Picnic at Baines' Baobabs	Jack's Camp

REPUBLIC OF ZIMBABWE

Facts at a Glance

Capital	Harare
Size	390 308 sq km
Population	11m
Currency	1 Zimbabwean dollar = 100 cents
Average Temperature	Summer min 16°C/max 26°C
– Harare	Winter min 7°C/max 21°C
Main Languages	Shona, Ndebele, English
Main Religions	Christianity, Indigenous Beliefs
Time Zone	GMT+2

Geographical Outline

Zimbabwe is a landlocked country situated in the south-eastern region of Africa. It is bordered to the north-west by Zambia, to the north-east and east by Mozambique, to the south by South Africa and to the south-west by Botswana. The country's main geological feature is the Great Dyke that runs from north to south for some 530km and is the source of many of the country's minerals. Altitudes range from 500m in the northern Zambezi Valley to 1 500m in the Highveld, dropping to around 300m in the south-east Lowveld region. Mountain ranges to be found within the Eastern Highlands region of the country are the Chimanimani and Inyanga, including Mount Inyangani, Zimbabwe's highest peak, standing at 2 592m. Two important rivers are the Zambezi, bordering Zambia to the north, and the Limpopo, which forms the southern boundary with South Africa. Lake Kariba, situated in the north-west of the land forms part of the border with Zambia.

The country's vegetation is a mixture of Mopane woodlands in the low altitude areas of the north and south, teak forests around Hwange National Park area and montane grasslands in the Eastern Highlands.

Introduction

The Region

Zimbabwe is considered by many to be one of Africa's most beautiful holiday destinations. It has a wealth of spectacular scenery and a variety of diverse tourist attractions, such as Victoria Falls, Lake Kariba, Great Zimbabwe (ruins) and the Eastern Highlands. It is renowned for its wildlife safaris, fishing, golf, adventure activities such as white water rafting, and its fascinating history and rich cultural heritage that can be experienced at such sights as the ruins of the ancient city of Great Zimbabwe.

The Economy

Zimbabwe's major industries are agriculture, mining, manufacturing and tourism. Tobacco is the nation's most important crop, followed by cotton and oil-seeds. Cattle farming is another main agricultural pursuit.

Important minerals are gold, emeralds, chrome ore and asbestos. Manufacturing is well developed and includes food, beverages, chemicals and textiles.

The Importance of Tourism

Tourism is considered to be of significant importance in Zimbabwe, generating foreign revenue and providing employment. It is one of Africa's most popular tourist destinations attracting over a million visitors annually. However, despite the obvious appeal of the region, it is not a mass-tourist destination because the country embraces the idea that tourism and the environment must continue to complement each other in a progressive and sustainable manner.

Climate

Zimbabwe's daytime summer (October–April) temperatures average between 25°–30°C, with warm evenings. Winter days (May–September) are generally dry and sunny with temperatures averaging between 15°–20°C. The temperature in low-lying areas such as Victoria Falls, Hwange, Kariba and the Zambezi Valley, is usually considerably warmer than the rest of the country. The rainy season lasts from November to March.

Transportation and Accessibility

Road

Surfaced highways link the nation's capital, Harare, with Bulawayo, Hwange, Victoria Falls, Kariba, the Eastern Highlands and the Lowveld. Normal two-wheel-drive vehicles are adequate for most of the country's roads, however, roads in the wilderness areas require four-wheel-drive vehicles. The Automobile Association of Zimbabwe is well represented throughout the country.

There is a good express inter-city coach service available between most major cities and luxury coaches run between Harare and Bulawayo, and Bulawayo and Victoria Falls.

Car hire companies are well represented in Zimbabwe's main centres and tourist destinations. Car hire is available with or without chauffeurs.

Tourism Destinations Southern Africa

Beitbridge	Bulawayo	Chimanimani	Chiredzi	Francistown	Gweru	Harare	Hwange	Kadoma	Kariba	KweKwe	Masvingo	Mutare	Nyanga	Rusape	Victoria Falls	Zvishavane
Beitbridge																
322	Bulawayo															
566	560	Chimanimani														
296	480	480	Chiredzi													
518	196	756	676	Francistown												
496	164	463	383	360	Gweru											
580	441	312	494	637	277	Harare										
610	288	848	768	484	452	729	Hwange									
604	299	598	518	495	135	142	567	Kadoma								
949	801	781	863	1006	646	369	1098	511	Kariba							
532	227	626	446	423	63	214	515	72	583	KweKwe						
286	280	280	200	476	183	294	568	318	663	246	Masvingo					
585	579	150	499	775	482	262	867	404	631	476	299	Mutare				
692	704	257	606	900	546	269	992	411	638	483	406	107	Nyanga			
678	610	243	592	806	446	169	898	311	538	383	392	93	100	Rusape		
761	439	999	919	636	603	880	198	738	1249	666	719	1018	1143	1049	Victoria Falls	
373	183	377	297	379	119	391	471	254	760	182	97	396	589	489	622	Zvishavane

▷ *Distances are measured in kilometres*

Border Crossings

The main border crossings into Zimbabwe are as follows.

Botswana: Ramokawebana Road (06:00–20:00)
Mozambique: Nyama-Panda (06:00–18:00), Forbes-Mutare (06:00–18:00)
South Africa: Beit Bridge (05:30–22:30)
Zambia: Victoria Falls (06:00–20:00), Kariba (06:00–18:00), Chirundu (06:18:00)
Zimbabwe/Botswana/Namibia/Zambia meet at Kazangula Road (06:00–18:00)

Air

Several international carriers, in addition to Air Zimbabwe, fly directly into Harare. Connections can be made through Johannesburg in South Africa. Air Zimbabwe and Zimbabwe Express operate both nationally and regionally to all the major centres. Airports are located at Harare, Bulawayo and Victoria Falls and charter flights are available throughout the country.

Rail

Zimbabwe has a good internal rail network as well as links to South Africa and Zambia.

Several companies offer luxury steam train safaris throughout Zimbabwe:

Train de Luxe

Services have recently been established at Victoria Falls in fully refurbished authentic steam trains. The Train de Luxe service operates the Zambezi Express between Victoria Falls and Hwange and the Zambezi Special between Victoria Falls and Bulawayo.

Rovos Rail–Pride of Africa

Rovos Rail offers luxury train safaris to Victoria Falls from Pretoria in South Africa via Mafikeng or Beit Bridge, with an excursion in Bulawayo.

The Blue Train

The Blue Train operates a two-night luxury service between Victoria Falls and Pretoria.

Boat

Houseboats are available for hire from registered charter companies at Lake Kariba. Several companies also offer cruises on the lake, including the traditional Mississippi-style paddle steamer, the Southern Belle.

Visa Requirements

Most visitors to Zimbabwe may enter for periods of up to six months with only a valid passport, a return ticket and/or proof of sufficient funds to cover the intended period of the visit. Although many nationalities do not require a visa to enter the county, South African citizens do. A visa may be obtained from the Zimbabwe High Commission.

Currency Restrictions

Visitors to Zimbabwe are allowed to bring up to Z$250 in cash and any amount of foreign currency in bank notes or travellers' cheques into the country. The total amount brought in must be declared at Customs on entry, otherwise the incumbent will only be allowed to exit the country with the equivalent of US$200 at the end of the visit.

There is an airport departure tax of US$20 to pay when leaving the country by air. The necessary revenue stamp may be bought at the airport or at any post office.

Accommodation

Hotel accommodation throughout Zimbabwe is graded on a 5-star system and is registered with the Tourist Board. Accommodation options range from luxury hotel and game lodges to camping and caravan facilities. Several of the hotels offer a host of sport and leisure activities and the numerous luxury private game lodges in various bush settings, provide superb game viewing. Many of the top hotels have excellent conference facilities.

Historic Highlights

Evidence of Stone Age Man in the region can be seen at the thousands of rock art sites situated throughout the country, especially within the Matobo National Park and around Harare.

Between 1250 and 1450 the ancestors of the modern Shona society established Great Zimbabwe which became the wealthiest and most powerful trading society in south-eastern Africa.

During the mid-19th century Ndebele raiders from the south gained a foothold in Zimbabwe and established their capital at Bulawayo.

In 1890 European explorers, missionaries and hunters moved into the area, establishing the country of Rhodesia as part of the British Empire.

In 1965 the then Prime Minister of Rhodesia declared unilateral independence from Britain.

Following the ten-year War of Independence, Robert Mugabe was elected as President in 1980.

Health

Precautions against malaria are advisable if visiting the low-lying areas of the country such as Victoria Falls, Kariba, Hwange and the Zambezi Valley. Due to the presence of bilharzia in some of the country's rivers and dams, it is not advisable to swim or to drink the water. Safe drinking water is available in towns and hotels.

Emergency medical help is provided throughout the country by Medical Air Rescue Service (MARS), which offers emergency ground and air response. Information can be obtained through their offices in Harare.

Population

Zimbabwe is made up of several different ethnic groups. The most predominant are the Shona and Ndebele who have retained many of their customs and traditions, such as the art of story telling. Much of what is known of their culture has been passed down in this way through the generations. A great deal of their customs are based on religious beliefs.

Social and Cultural Profile

Although the country's modern centres, such as Harare and Bulawayo, are now connected to the rest of the world by satellite television and international media, only a small percentage of the nation's people live in the city. Despite the changes brought about by high-tech city living, life for the people in the rural areas carries on much the same as it always has with close-knit communities centred in village life.

Many of the people of European descent are involved in farming, mining and various entrepreneurial pursuits.

Art

Traditional Zimbabwean crafts include pottery, carving, textiles and basketry. Many local representations of visual art are a mixture of African and European styles.

Shona Sculpture

Shona sculpture has evolved over the past 30 years and has today become an integral part of Zimbabwean art. Most sculptures are styled after African folklore and depict animals, gods, totems and spirits. Well-known sculptors include John Takawira, Henry Munyaradzi and Bernard Matemera.

Literature

Most of the nation's early literature was produced by the country's European population and includes works by Gertrude Page and Cynthia Stockley. Well-known novels set in Zimbabwe are *The Grass is Singing* by Doris Lessing, and *A Falcon Flies* and *Men of Men*, both by Wilbur Smith. The first Shona book, *Feso* by S. Mutswairo was published in 1956 and the first Ndebele novel *Umthawakazi* by P.S. Mahlangu was published in 1957. Other popular works by Zimbabwean writers include Tsitsi Dangarembga's *Nervous Conditions* — set in eastern Zimbabwe during the 1960s, and *Coming in the Dry Season* by Charles Mungoshi.

Music

Music is an integral part of the Zimbabwean culture. Traditional instruments that form the base of their music include the *marimba* (xylophone), the *mbira* (thumb piano), the *ngoma* (drum), as well as several types of maracas, flutes and bells, including the *mujejeje* or stone bells.

There are many music venues throughout the country and information is available in the local newspapers.

Religion

Christianity is one of the main religions in Zimbabwe, however many people practise a hybrid of Christianity and traditional beliefs. Another important traditional form of religion, which has existed in the region since the time of Great Zimbabwe, is the Mwari Cult, which entails ancestor worship.

Cuisine

Traditional Zimbabwe cuisine is a mixture of African and British dishes. Staple foods include white maize-meal porridge and meat. The country is one of the world's great beef producers and it is therefore plentiful. Chicken, goat, mutton and game are also eaten, as is fish around Lake Kariba, and trout in the Eastern Highlands region. Popular fruit and vegetables include maize, gem squash, tomatoes, pumpkin, bananas, papayas and mangoes. Preferred beverages include Malawi Shandy, which is made of ginger beer, Angostura bitters and soda water, served with ice and lemon, or Rock Shandy which consists of the same ingredients except the ginger beer is replaced by lemonade and Mazoe Orange, an orange cordial. Popular alcoholic drinks include lager, wine and spirits and the local brew *chibuku*, drunk mainly in shebeens or township beer halls.

Festivals and Events

Festivals and events celebrated in Zimbabwe include New Year's Day, Easter, Independence Day on 18 April, Workers Day on 1 May, Africa Day on 25 May, Heroes Day, 11 August, Defence Forces Day, 12 August, National Unity Day, 22 December, Christmas Day, 25 December and Boxing Day, 26 December.

Sport and Leisure Facilities

Sport is something of a national obsession in Zimbabwe and plays an important role in the social calendar. Football matches are the most popular event, although cricket, rugby, horseracing and polo also have a large following. Numerous organisations offer tours specialising in activities such as bird watching, fishing, elephant-back safaris, horse trails, river rafting, canoeing, river boarding and wildlife safaris. Details are available at the various tourist information offices and the Zimbabwe Council for Tourism.

Wildlife Safaris

Numerous tour operators and individuals offer wildlife safaris in the many national parks and reserves. Safari options include walking, horse riding or travelling in open vehicles, and are somewhat determined by the status of the park, which can range from luxury game lodge to basic rustic accommodation. Private guides and organised trips can be arranged through local tourism offices.

Birding Safaris

With some 664 species recorded within the country, Zimbabwe is a favourite venue for bird watching. Several companies offer birding safaris into various habitats. Certain species which are rarely seen elsewhere in the world, such as the *Chirinda apalis* found in the high-level mist belt forests of the Eastern Highlands, are found within the country.

Elephant-back Safaris

Morning and afternoon elephant-back safaris operate from Victoria Falls. Guests are given an opportunity to gain a better insight into the day-to-day life of these animals, prior to riding along the game viewing trails.

▷ *On safari – riding an elephant*

Hunting Safaris

Several companies offer hunting safaris across the country and information can be obtained at the tourist information offices.

Fishing

Fishing can be enjoyed at popular venues such as Lake Kariba for catching tiger fish, and the Eastern Highlands for trout fishing.

Golf

Zimbabwe is well known for its golf courses, many of which are located in spectacularly beautiful surroundings. Some of the clubs have 18-hole courses and most extend a friendly welcome to visitors. Favourite venues include the 18-hole course at the Elephant Hills Hotel on the banks of the Zambezi River, and the 18-hole Leopard Rock Golf Course set in Upper Bvumba in the Eastern Highlands.

White Water Rafting and Canoeing

The gorges below the Victoria Falls are considered to be some of the finest white water rafting locales in the world. Experience is not a prerequisite but you must be fit.

Canoeing safaris are available in areas such as the Upper and Lower Zambezi regions as well as through the Mana Pools National Park.

▷ *The thrill of white water rafting*

Bungee Jumping

The jump off the Victoria Falls Bridge is one of the highest in the world.

Traditional Dancing

Traditional Dancing can be experienced at several venues in Zimbabwe, such as the Victoria Falls Hotel, Elephant Hills Hotel and Boma Restaurant at Victoria Falls.

Conservation and Eco-Tourism

Zimbabwe is well known for its role in environmental conservation. Its CAMPFIRE – Communal Areas Management Programme for Indigenous Resources – project was established in 1989. It promotes utilisation of the land's natural resources in the interests of conservation of the environment and to assist in the upliftment of rural communities. Projects include communities generating income and employment through the leasing of sites for tourism facilities; cultural villages; and live animal sales where excess stock of wildlife species are sold to other communities or commercial wildlife breeders.

The Chipangali Wildlife Orphanage near Bulawayo provides a sanctuary for orphaned and injured wild animals. Species found at the centre include lion, jackal, wild dog, leopard and caracal.

Wildlife Parks and Nature Reserves

Victoria Falls National Park

The Victoria Falls National Park encompasses the Falls and surrounding area. There is a paved pathway along the edge of the waterfalls leading to the various lookout points and affording awe-inspiring views of the five separate falls – Rainbow Falls, Horseshoe Falls, Devil's Cataract, Main Falls and the Eastern Cataract.

▷ *Victoria Falls*

Zambezi National Park

Situated alongside the Zambezi River a short distance from Victoria Falls is the Zambezi National Park. There is an excellent game-viewing site at the Njako Pan and several attractive picnic spots. Accommodation within the park consists of riverside chalets.

Hwange National Park

Set aside for the conservation of wildlife in its natural habitat, the 14 000 sq km national park is home to over 100 different species of animal and 400 species of bird. There are some 482km of game-viewing roads throughout the park where visitors can experience some of the greatest concentrations of game in Africa. Activities include morning and evening game drives and game walks with professional guides. Accommodation is provided in three camps – Main Camp, Robins Camp and Sinamatella – and consists of lodges, chalets, tents or caravans. Luxury safari lodges, such as Hwange Safari Lodge and Sable Valley Lodge, are also located within the area.

Mana Pools National Park

The Mana Pools National Park covers an area of 2 000 sq km and is one of Zimbabwe's National Heritage Sites. The great Zambezi River meanders through this ancient floodplain forming small pools over this vast expanse of land. There is a wealth of bird life and animals within the region, especially during the dry months of September and October. Accommodation is available at the Rukomechni and Chikwenya Lodges as well as at caravan and camp sites, or in one of the surrounding luxury safari lodges overlooking the park.

Matobo National Park

The Matobo National Park is situated 53km south of Bulawayo and covers an area of 43 200 ha. The park, known for its fascinating rock formations is home to the ancient Matobo Hills, as well as historical sites such as the grave of Cecil John Rhodes and numerous San rock paintings. Accommodation within the park consists of chalets and caravan and camp sites.

Nyanga National Park

Most of the land that makes up the Nyanga National Park was a gift to the nation from Cecil John Rhodes. It is situated in the northernmost part of the Eastern Highlands and is an area rich in bird life and game such as kudu, wildebeest and leopard. The country's highest mountain, Inyangani, is located within the region, as are the Nyanga Ancient Ruins, Nyazengu Nature Reserve, Pungwe Gorge, Honde Valley, Mutarazi National Park and Mutarazi Falls, Africa's second highest waterfall. The villages of Nyanga, Troutbeck and Juliasdale are linked by good gravel roads and offer hotel accommodation, trout-fishing and horse-riding facilities. The park's campsites are located at Nyangome and Mutarazi.

Gonarezhou National Park

The Gonarezhou National Park is located in the hot, dry region of the south-east Lowveld, 260km from Masvingo along the Mozambique border. It has abundant bird life and is home to elephant, buffalo, lion, wild dog, suni, nyala, pangolin, Liechtenstein's hartebeest and roan antelope.

The park is divided into two sections – Chipinda Pools and Mabalauta. Accommodation in the Chipinda Pools area consists of camping facilities at Chipinda Pools and at Chinguli; in the Mabalauta region there are camp and caravan sites, and thatched chalets at Swimuwini. Picnic sites and hides, where overnight camping is permitted, are located at Benji Viewpoint and Fishans Picnic Site in the Chipinda Pools area, and at Manyanda Pan and Rossi Pools Viewpoint in Mabalauta.

Chimanimani National Park

The Chimanimani National Park is situated in the eastern region of the country close to the Mozambique border. This rugged wilderness area is a favourite venue for hikers.

Matusadona National Park

Positioned between the Ume and Sanyati rivers on the shores of Lake Kariba, the Matusadona National Park can be reached by road, boat or air. The park covers an area of 1 407km of wild, rugged and often inaccessible terrain only suitable for four-wheel-drive vehicles; its game-viewing roads are closed during the rainy season. Accommodation consists of three exclusive camps at Ume, Muuyu and Mbalabala and facilities for camping at Tashinga and Sanyati.

Tourist Attractions

Harare

The nation's capital is situated high on the central plateau. Places worth visiting within the city include the National Art Gallery, the Queen Victoria Museum, and the Queen Victoria National Library. Shopping opportunities are plentiful and local craft centres sell a wide range of artefacts including wonderful Shona sculptures.

Restaurants abound, offering both local and international cuisine. The city's bustling nightlife offers music at many of its hotels, bars and nightclubs.

Attractions outside the city include the Tengenenge Art Community, which houses more than 17 000 sculptures, and the Mukuvisi Woodlands.

Victoria Falls

Victoria Falls is where the mighty Zambezi River plunges headlong into a deep gorge. It is one of the natural wonders of the world, and a World Heritage Site. The Falls, the country's greatest tourist attraction, are known by the local people as *Mosi-oa-Tunya* (the smoke that thunders), describing the noise and the spray cloud that is visible from several kilometres away.

The first foreigner to report sighting the Falls to the outside world was the Christian missionary and explorer, David Livingstone, who named them after Queen Victoria of England.

▷ *Statue of David Livingstone in the Victoria Falls National Park*

Victoria Falls and the surrounding area have much to offer. Dawn, lunch and sundowner cruises on the Zambezi give visitors a chance to enjoy the river whilst spotting wildlife along the riverbank. Guided walks through the surrounding indigenous bush and rain forest, game drives into the nearby parks, or a visit to the Big Tree, an ancient baobab estimated to be over 1 500 years old, are some of the tourist options. There are scheduled helicopter flights, such as the Flight of Angels that gives a bird's eye view of the Falls, or the Zambezi Heli Safari over the Falls and the Zambezi National Park. Adventure sports such as white water rafting, bungee jumping, and canoeing are all well represented.

Other places worth visiting are the Zambezi Wildlife Sanctuary and Crocodile Ranch where animals can be viewed at close quarters, and a variety of locally made handicrafts may be purchased from the curio shop; and the craft village, where the local people come to sell their handicrafts.

Popular hotels include the Victoria Falls Hotel, built in 1904 and still considered to be one of the most romantic venues in the country; the Elephant Hills Hotel, renowned for its beautiful 18-hole golf course; and the Victoria Falls Safari Lodge overlooking the Zambezi National Park, with uninterrupted views of the surrounding bush and on-site waterhole.

▷ *A view from Victoria Falls Safari Lodge*

Lake Kariba

The Kariba Dam was completed in 1958, creating an inland-sea of some 200km in length and 40km in breadth at its widest. The dam provides the country with much-needed hydro-electricity as well as a recreation area for fishing, water-skiing and sailing, in a lovely setting of mountains, forests and bushveld. There is an abundance of game viewing in the area, which can be appreciated from either a boat on the water or safari vehicle along the shore. The town of Kariba is situated at the end of the dam and offers a variety of accommodation, restaurants and entertainment.

Eastern Highlands

Extending some 300km from north to south on the country's eastern border with Mozambique, are the rolling hills and spectacular mountain scenery known as the Eastern Highlands. Popular pastimes well catered for in the region include hiking, trout fishing, golfing, bowls and horse riding.

Places of particular interest include the volcanic peaks of Chimanimani, the Vumba Botanical Gardens close to Mutare, and the Nyanga National Park.

Bulawayo

Situated in the south-western part of the country, Bulawayo is the nation's second major city. Within the city are many fine examples of Victorian buildings, which have been maintained as heritage sites. Places worth visiting include the Natural History Museum, the Railway Museum, the Bulawayo Art Gallery, the Mzilikazi Art and Craft Centre and the Amakhosi Cultural Centre which offers regular performances of traditional drama, music and singing.

Historic Sites

Great Zimbabwe

Situated less than 30km from the south-eastern town of Masvingo are the ruins of Great Zimbabwe. The ruins of the ancient city, built between AD1250 and AD1450 by the ancestors of modern Shona-Zimbabweans, are the nation's most important historic site.

Khami (Kame) Ruins

Khami (Kame) Ruins mark the site of the powerful Rozwi kings who ruled the area for over 500 years. The site of the ruins is fairly extensive and the adjoining land has been transformed into a nature reserve where visitors may drive, picnic and walk.

▷ *The ruins of Great Zimbabwe*

Activity

Identify six main attractions that you would recommend to a first-time visitor to Zimbabwe. Give reasons for your selection.

References

Ballard, Sebastian & Linton, Rupert. 1996. *South Africa Handbook*. Bath, UK: Footprint Handbooks.

Camerapix. 1994. *Spectrum Guide to Namibia*. Cape Town: Struik.

Elliott, Aubrey. 1989. *The Ndebele Art and Culture*. Cape Town: Struik.

Heale, Jay. 1981. *They made this land*. Johannesburg: Ad. Donker.

Levitas, Ben. *Ethnology – An introduction to the peoples and cultures of southern Africa*. Cape Town: Oxford University Press.

Mandela, Nelson. 1994. *Long Walk to Freedom*. Randburg, South Africa: MacDonald Purnell.

McIntyre, Chris & Atkins, Simon. 1991. *Guide to Namibia and Botswana*. Bradt Publications UK: Distributed in South Africa by SA Media Publications, Sandton.

Mugubane, P. 1998. *Vanishing Cultures of South Africa*. Cape Town: Struik.

Satour. *The 1997 Factfiler*.

Swaney, Deanna. 1992. *Zimbabwe/Botswana/Namibia – A Travel Survival Kit*. Lonely Planet Publications.

The Automobile Association of South Africa. 1996. (2nd ed.) *Off the Beaten Track - Selected day drives in southern Africa*. Cape Town: AA The Motorist Publications.

The Automobile Association of South Africa. 1995. *Places to Visit in Southern Africa*. Cape Town: AA The Motorist Publications.

Van der Post, Laurens. 1958. *Lost World of the Kalahari*. London: Penguin.